But I Didn't
Want A
DIVORCE

BOOKS BY ANDRE BUSTANOBY—
You Can Change Your Personality
But I Didn't Want A Divorce

But I Didn't Want A DIVORCE

Putting Your Life Back Together

André Bustanoby

**ZONDERVAN
PUBLISHING HOUSE** OF THE ZONDERVAN CORPORATION
GRAND RAPIDS, MICHIGAN 49506

BUT I DIDN'T WANT A DIVORCE
Copyright © 1978 by Andre Bustanoby

Library of Congress Cataloging in Publication Data

Bustanoby, Andre.
   . . . But I didn't want a divorce.

   1. Divorce.   2. Divorce—Biblical training.
3. Divorcees.   4. Remarriage.   I. Title.
HQ823.B87   301.42'84   78-15531
ISBN 0-310-22170-6 cloth
ISBN 0-310-22171-4 paper

Printed in the United States of America

Contents

Preface

In spite of your religious convictions and your commitment to marriage, you may find yourself involved in a divorce suit—either by your own choice or completely against your will.

As a marriage counselor, I have found that there is a naïve notion, especially among Christians and others with strong religious beliefs, that having strong religious convictions against divorce and wanting a marriage to work are enough to make it work. But that just isn't true. For any marriage to work, both spouses must be committed to the relationship and willing to do whatever is necessary to make it work. Willingness on the part of one is not enough.

I am writing to those who, though they may have desired to remain married, have been forced by the actions of their spouse to separate or divorce. Their mental health and physical safety depended on such a decision.

Finally, I am also writing to those who, in spite of their strong convictions against divorce and remarriage, do so only because their marriage has died.

This book attempts to answer the following questions in their logical sequence. In view of the demise of your marriage, what does the Bible say about divorce? Given the reality of your divorce, what about the practical matters of the emotional pain, your children, and the law? Does the Bible permit remarriage after a divorce and, if it does, is remarriage a wise move for you?

Let's take an important and necessary look at the subjects of divorce and remarriage. Things have gone beyond the point of return. Whether you are the unwilling party to a divorce suit or are initiating suit because you feel you must, the painful subject must be faced. Your spiritual, emotional, and physical survival depend on it.

But I Didn't
Want A
DIVORCE

CHAPTER 1

. . . But I Didn't Want a Divorce

It may seem grossly unfair that you can be divorced by your spouse even though you want your marriage to work. Yet, if your spouse is determined to divorce you, a divorce can become final. More and more states are amending their divorce laws to permit "no-fault" divorce. In "no-fault" divorce, either party may file for separation, and after a prescribed waiting period the divorce is granted. Lawmakers are no longer willing to forbid divorce to those who want it.

No matter how opposed to divorce you and your church may be and no matter how much you may want to stay married, you may, like Drew and Kay, become a divorce statistic this year.

Drew seemed to have so much going for him and seemed able to solve almost any problem. He was an elder in his church, was professionally and financially successful, and had all the material trappings of success. But Drew was desperate, willing to do anything to keep his marriage alive; nothing he tried had changed Kay's determination to divorce him.

Over a period of thirteen years, he had sought marriage counseling many times. At first Kay cooperated, and the counseling seemed to help. But before long, they were at odds again. Kay lost interest in her two boys and did not even care about their physical welfare. When they left for school, they usually had gotten themselves together the best they could. Drew, who left for work early, was never sure if the boys had eaten breakfast before they left. Then, as Kay lost interest in the home, it became a pigsty. Her only interest was the fun she had with her two divorced girlfriends. They made the rounds of the local watering holes, not to pick up men, but just to "live it up." Kay's day started at 6:00 P.M., when she got out of bed to get ready for her evening out, and ended somewhere between 2:00 A.M. and 4:00 A.M., when she returned home.

Over the years, she had told all the marriage counselors the same thing. At age seventeen, right out of high school, she married the boy that her church and parents approved of because she was told that it was the "right" move. She then got down to the business of being active in her church, being a devoted homemaker, and having children. But now, at age thirty, she was bailing out of her marriage.

> I'm not going to spend the rest of my life like I've spent the last thirteen years—the duty of motherhood, the duty of homemaking, the duty of being a good wife, the duty of being a good church member. I'm tired of duty. I want to have fun! Every day I spend in this house reminds me of my *duty*. I'm sick of it. My duty as a girl was to be obedient to my parents and do nothing that would embarrass them or the church. My duty in high school was to get good grades. What happiness has all this devotion to duty gotten me in thirty years?

Kay's anger seethed; she stopped speaking and looked suspiciously at me as if I were trying to shove her into the mold of duty. Even my expressions of understanding and caring were met with hostility. Unwilling to be trapped in a life of duty, desperate to be free, Kay filed for divorce shortly after our meeting.

Why wasn't Kay willing to make her marriage work? Emotional immaturity was the key reason. A successful marriage involves more than just a couple's determination to make it work. Within a marriage, both people must have learned beforehand how to accept responsibility. This sense of responsibility is not formed overnight. Rather, it's built into the character of a child day by day. At some point in the child's development, he must realize that responsibility is not merely the restriction of fun. He must learn that responsibility is the means to the end of true happiness and fulfillment.

Drew also had to understand the nature of responsibility before he could accept Kay's actions. No one could give her a crash course in responsibility. The training she had missed in the process of growing up could not be supplied through marriage counseling. Plainly irresponsible, Kay had no desire to change. Divorce offered her an opportunity to escape the responsibilities that marriage had imposed on her. It's easy to understand why she wanted nothing to do with marriage counseling: it threatened to entrap her in responsibility.

What could a counselor say to Drew? Was he to be told that, as an elder in his church, he shouldn't let something like this happen? Was he to be told that his church frowns on divorce and that he had better do something? He had tried to do something for thirteen years and was beginning to destroy himself by intense introspection. Although he had done everything he could to make his marriage work, he still felt that he should resign his position as an elder. Perhaps he had contributed to the demise of his marriage, but at this late date, self-flagellation and the desire to make his marriage work at any cost would not change a thing. Kay had filed for a divorce and that was that!

PASSIVE AND PUZZLED

When I first met Frieda, she seemed friendly and easygoing. But from her doctor's referral slip, I knew that she was in deep trouble. She had just about every physical malady that nervous tension could produce, but she kept her tension buried under a calm exterior.

She began our discussion by explaining that she didn't understand why she couldn't cope. "I have read scores of books about coping with anxiety and depression," she stated, "and have attended every marriage and successful-living seminar that came to town." But she still was having problems and was beginning to doubt her faith. "I really wonder if Christ is the answer," she said slowly, looking at her feet. "He doesn't seem to be answering my prayers."

What was Frieda's problem? Why was she so uptight? She really didn't seem to know, unless of course her husband's affair had something to do with it. The matter-of-fact way in which she unfolded the story of her husband's infidelity was surprising, to say the least. Her husband had been seeing a single girl for about a year, and only a week before Frieda's visit, the girlfriend had a baby. When asked, her husband had admitted that it was his child.

Frieda was puzzled. She couldn't understand why she had taken the news of the birth so badly. As she continued to speak, I learned that she was no stranger to infidelity. Her husband had had many affairs over their eight years of marriage, and this was the second child he had fathered out of wedlock. "What's wrong with me?" Frieda asked, after she finished talking. I resisted the temptation to tell her that she had taken leave of her senses by putting up with eight years of infidelity and destroying her health by concealing her feelings.

Bucky, Frieda's husband, wasn't about to talk with me. When I called him to ask if he'd come in with his wife, he immediately let me know what he thought about "shrinks" and told me to stay out of his business.

Bucky's response really made a great deal of sense. Why should he permit anyone to ruin a life style that offered him a cook, laundress, and mother for his children, as well as Frieda's permission to maintain countless concubines?

Even though Bucky wouldn't cooperate, I still had a responsibility to make Frieda realize that most of her problems were due to her incredible passivity and lack of critical discernment. She had to see that, although she might passively absorb abuse, her stomach and every nerve in her body were going to argue back. On the other hand, I feared that if I helped her develop assertiveness and outrage at her husband's behavior, she would leave him. And that's exactly what happened.

Even during the divorce proceedings, she had moments when she wished that she hadn't "stirred things up." "It's going to be a lonely life," she said slowly, "and I don't know if I'm going to be able to make it on my own. He always took care of the car—getting it serviced, new tires, and all that. What's more, I don't have the faintest idea how to do an income tax return. And he did keep the house in repair. Sometimes I wonder if a bad relationship is better than none at all."

Frieda was tempted many times to go back to Bucky. But he finally made the decision for her. After the year of voluntary separation, the divorce went through and Bucky married one of his girlfriends. And dear, sensitive Frieda? What would she do now? Bucky had closed the door to any hope that they would ever get back together again. Frieda was now single and, like it or not, she had to get on with the business of living.

The Low-Priority Spouse

Twenty-five years is a long time to be married. Most people assume that a couple married that long would have most of their problems ironed out. Ellen thought so too. She and Frank had been married for twenty-five years, had three children, and even a grandchild. She was aware that Frank was unhappy, but she was totally unprepared for his announcement that he wanted a divorce.

When she came to me, she was baffled and hurt. She had looked back over her years of marriage again and again, trying to figure out what had gone wrong. During her visit, Ellen said that Frank was willing to talk with me, but he had already told her that his mind was made up.

Frank, a sober and reasonable man, poured out his thoughts to me. He professed to be a Christian, and his decision to divorce Ellen was causing him great conflict. He believed he was doing wrong by divorcing her, but felt he had to go through with it.

What had gone wrong? Nothing big—just twenty-five years of unrewarding marriage. Yes, there were little things that bothered him. "Ellen was too preoccupied with the children and a lot of other things to have much time for me," he confessed. "For most of our marriage, I recognized that I came last on her list of priorities. But I didn't really let it bother me

/ 15

much at the time. I guess I felt pretty self-sufficient. But now," Frank continued, "I'm forty-five. I've lived half of my life less than happy. I don't want the rest of my life to be like that. My love for Ellen just isn't there any more, and it's time to bury our dead marriage."

I called Ellen into the room. When Frank shared with her what he had told me, she was hurt. "Why didn't you tell me years ago that your feelings for me were dying and that you felt you came last in my life?"

Frank admitted that he had been wrong in keeping silent. But the fact was that he no longer loved her. Yes, he would take care of her, and the terms of the divorce would be liberal. But he had no desire to make the marriage work. Like it or not, marriage was over for Ellen. Yes, it would take time for the divorce to go through. If she fought it, it would take three years. If she agreed to voluntary separation, it would take one year. But Frank wanted to get out of the marriage, and that was that.

Ellen finally agreed to a voluntary separation. She hoped that if she were kind to Frank during the period of separation, he would see the light and want a reconciliation. Even when Frank started dating again, she did her best to be nice to him. But her life fell apart when she heard through a friend that after their year of separation, Frank was filing for a divorce so that he could remarry. Like Frieda, Ellen had religious scruples against divorce. Yet, despite her convictions and her willingness to change, she became a single person with no hope of reconciliation to her former husband.

Things in Common

Two things are common to these three cases. All of the people involved, including Bucky, professed to be Christians. In each case, one spouse was determined to get a divorce, and did so, over the objection of the other spouse. Regardless of their religious convictions against divorce, the divorced spouses had to make new lives as single people. In two of the cases, remarriage closed the door to any hope of reconciliation. The reality of a single life became very clear in those situations; if religious scruples forbade remarriage, it meant living as single people for the rest of their lives.

I would be unrealistic in addressing the question of divorce and remarriage without taking note of the many Christians who divorce and remarry for no other reason than the death of their marriage and the appearance of someone else who promises new life. Such Christians feel particularly alienated from the church and estranged from God.

The following letter I received from a client offers insight into the incredible pain of Christians who are caught between religious scruples against divorce and remarriage and the opportunity to feel alive again in a new marriage. Of course, I've changed the letter to protect the writer.

> Dear Andy,
>
> I feel that I owe you an apology for not being completely honest with you when Hank and I came for counseling last Tuesday. You asked me if another man was in the picture, and I tried to avoid telling you what I'm telling you now. I wasn't ready then.
>
> You probably guessed that someone else is in the picture. In fact, I must confess that I'm deeply in love with another man. I don't want to hurt Hank, but at this point, I feel that Hank is just a friend and nothing more.
>
> Hank has never been communicative or expressed his feelings to any depth. Our relationship has been superficial from the beginning. I can't get sexually excited in a relationship like that.
>
> What adds to my negative feelings about Hank is that two years ago, when I realized that our marriage was in trouble, I asked Hank to go to a Christian marriage seminar that had come to town. He wasn't interested, so I went by myself. The seminar made me realize how much I was missing in my marriage. I also tried to get Hank to go to a marriage counselor. But all my attempts were met with indifference. He kept saying that we didn't have any problems.
>
> At this time, I began a project at work and in one of the teams was a man whom I grew to admire. He was open, communicative, complimentary of my work and of me as a person. But above all, he seemed to be able to read my moods and my mind. For the first time in many years, I felt like a worthwhile person and that I was alive.
>
> I think that I love and respect him even more because he has

never tried to make any sexual advances. He is a truly caring person. Whenever I go home to Hank, the difference is so startling that I get terribly depressed.

I want to love Hank and not this other man. But no matter what my mind says, the feelings are there. I'm becoming more and more angry at God and Hank, even though I shouldn't have these feelings either. But more and more, I find myself yelling at God, "I gave you and Hank a chance for two years to keep this from happening. Why didn't you do something before it was too late?"

Call it self-justification or rationalization if you will. But there's where I am. If I had to make a decision about my marriage right now, I'd leave.

I'm telling you this so you'll know what you're up against. I don't know if you can help. I'm afraid it's too late.

Sincerely,

Brenda

The outcome of the story is that Brenda eventually left Hank. Her divorce is now pending. Even though she wants to marry the other man, she has tremendous guilt feelings which stir even greater anger toward God and the church. It remains to be seen whether or not Brenda will remarry. But in any event, she needs to know that God and her brothers and sisters in Christ love her—and not in a condescending way. She needs the kind of love that says, "Brenda, I'm struggling too. My battle is different from yours, but I know you hurt, and I care. I need your caring too."

CHAPTER 2

Between Separation and Divorce

You feel as if you're in limbo. You're not divorced—yet. And you find it difficult to give up the hope that your marriage will work. Perhaps you have visited one or more marriage counselors, therapists, or doctors hoping that one of them might persuade your spouse that your marriage is worth saving. And your hope just won't die. Perhaps, even though the divorce papers have been served, you still are unwilling to give up hope.

LET GO OF YOUR SPOUSE

Such dedication to your marriage is praiseworthy, but it may not be good for you. Dedication to a dead marriage is much like holding onto a spouse who has died. Often clients tell me that they could accept the death of the spouse easier than a divorce. That may be true: there is a sense of rejection in divorce that is not found in death. But a person who tries to hang on when a marriage is over would probably do the same thing when a spouse died.

Mel Krantzler describes the loss of a spouse in divorce in similar terms. He writes:

> Divorce is an emotional crisis triggered by a sudden and unexpected loss. The death of a relationship is the first stage in a process in which the death is recognized, and the relationship is mourned and then laid to rest to make way for self-renewal. Intellectually, a newly separated person may deny being in crisis, but it is there to see in everything he or she does. Suddenly, normal ways of coping do not seem to work. Overnight the world has changed into a frightening question mark, and every-day life is out of control. Simple decisions are no longer manageable; even getting dressed in the morning is difficult and often not worth the effort.[1]

When faced with a divorce he doesn't want, a person follows a predictable pattern. Krantzler describes it this way:

> [There is] a separation shock which can equal in intensity the feelings evoked by the actual death of a husband or wife; and it sets in motion reactions similar to those which an actual death can cause: initial denial that the relationship has ended, producing at first a retreat into a fantasy life where it can still live on; powerful feelings of hostility and anger toward the absent person for having abandoned us to an intolerable life without him or her; pervasive feelings of guilt, internalized or projected, over things we did and didn't do during the relationship (and) a withdrawal from those parts of our past too painful to cope with (or too irrelevant to survive in our present lives).[2]

Many people never get beyond these reactions. They learn to endure life and believe that their withdrawn single state is the best they can hope for. Their lives become dead, since meaning and purpose are no longer things to enjoy and attain.

Krantzler advances the idea that far more adjustment to divorce must take place. He says that there must be "a gradual testing and retesting of reality; and an eventual letting-go from the influence of the past relationship so that a new life can begin."[3]

In chapter 7 I will deal with some of the specific emotions you will confront as you adjust to divorce. But in this chapter I want to deal with the importance of learning to "let go." This learning process begins with the realization that the relationship is dead. I don't mean to imply that a person receiving a divorce will succeed at letting go by the time the divorce is final. Krantzler points out that letting go doesn't happen until the divorced person is ready to accept the reality of being single and ready to develop the qualities he will need in his new life. Only then can he finally let go and emerge into the reality of single life.

DEVELOP A POSITIVE ATTITUDE

Often when I tell a client that he must let go of his relationship, he replies, "But how can I? I love him (or her) so much!" I don't want to be cold and clinical here, but I think that we need to look carefully at this emotion called "love." Just as it's possible to cultivate feelings of love for a person by repeated positive contact and positive mental images, it's possible also to learn to disengage yourself from that love, much in the same way that a person accepts the death of a spouse.

Many times a person who says he can't let go because of love doesn't realize that he may unwittingly be deceiving himself. Often the real emotion he feels is rejection. It's the old story that we often don't realize what we have until we're about to lose or have lost it. The desire to hang on may arise from an attempt to escape rejection, rather than a genuine expression of love. Of course, it's far more acceptable to say that we're hanging on because of love rather than a feeling of rejection. And "love" is also a far better motive to advance for hanging on. If we can hang on, we don't have to think about what we have done to contribute to the demise of the marriage—a guilt that is hard to bear. So we grieve about a love that we are about to lose.

Women often hang onto a relationship in the name of love when they really are hanging on for security. Men—especially competitive men—will hang on because they can't bear the thought of losing. They usually can buy, persuade, or browbeat their way to success. But this is one instance where they lose decisively.

Grieving over a love lost is also a way to indulge in self-pity and get positive responses from others. Or, if we don't get comfort from others, we use our grief as an excuse to stroke ourselves. When we are hurt emotionally, we naturally seek some kind of soothing stroke for our pain. But whenever we pull pity from others and ourselves, we slow down the healing process that we must go through and use our minds destructively. For example, a person who spends a great deal of time trying to figure out how to revive his dead marriage or lamenting over rejection will end up at a frustrated dead end. Such activity creates negative mental pictures. We may picture our former spouses living it up, for example, while we drag ourselves home to our drab little apartments.

Maxwell Maltz, author of *Psycho-Cybernetics*, and other writers have stressed the importance of using our minds constructively. We may not have direct control over how we feel, but we *do* have control over what we think. I'm not talking about controlling involuntary thoughts; I am speaking of what we should do after those involuntary thoughts enter our minds.

Let's say, for example, that the involuntary thought pops into your mind, *He's divorcing me; now my life is ruined.* You have a choice to make at this point. You can engage in self-pity—preventing the development of a positive mental attitude—or you can say to yourself, *The marriage is over, and the sooner I accept it the better I'll feel.* It helps to state this latter thought aloud. Whether you're alone in your car or at home, say it aloud, angrily and with emphasis. When you look at yourself in the mirror, don't say it with a pitiful expression on your face or in a pitiful tone of voice. Say it the way your best friend might say it to you when he or she is trying to snap you out of your self-pity.

I believe that Martin Luther had this principle in mind when he spoke of how he dealt with depression. He said, "Pray a lot, and get downright angry." Anger can be used constructively to combat self-pity, because it floods the body with adrenalin and makes you *feel* like doing something about your situation. It is hoped you can then direct your anger constructively toward getting up, going to visit a friend, or making new friends.

The same principle applies if you have the involuntary thought, *How will I take care of myself?* Again, you have the choice of either indulging in self-pity or angrily saying to yourself, *I'm not going to have a pity-party. By God's help, I am going to take care of myself, and if I don't have any more guts than to sit here and whine, then maybe I ought to dry up and blow away.*

Maltz advances a similar principle when he writes that the brain is a "goal-striving mechanism."[4] He offers the idea that when we fix a goal in our minds, either positive or negative, all the body's resources automatically muster themselves to accomplish that goal. If your goal is to let go of your spouse and begin a new life for yourself, you must keep this goal continually fixed in your mind and say it aloud. Conversely, you must refuse to poison your mind with the usual negative thinking, resentment, and self-pity that prevent healing after a divorce.

I'm not suggesting that you try to get over the pain of your divorce by "stuffing" your feelings—repressing them and pretending that they don't exist. They are very real, and if you repress them, they will show up in other ways. In chapter 9, I'll examine a therapeutic process that you can use to deal with unresolved, negative feelings. Right now, however, I want you to grasp firmly the fact that you must not indulge in self-pity and that you can change your feelings toward the divorce by developing a different mental attitude.

The Epistle to the Philippians calls for positive thinking and the abandonment of self-pity. The apostle Paul, writing from a prison cell, told the Philippians:

> Whatever is true, whatever is honorable, whatever is right, whatever is pure, whatever is lovely, whatever is of good repute; if there is any excellence, and if anything worthy of praise, let your mind dwell on these things. . . . and the God of peace shall be with you.[5]

It's interesting to note that the God of peace promises to be with us when we decide to think positively. I assume that the opposite is also true: if we don't think about positive things, the God of peace will not be with us.

You should apply the same concept of positive thinking to your prayer life. If your prayers have not changed your negative mood, it's probably because they have reinforced your negative thinking. It's one thing to tell God that you hurt and quite another thing to go on and on vividly describing your pain. If you ask God to help you pray positively, He will gradually turn your optimism and prayers toward positive thoughts about the future.

John Claypool focuses on the fact that this kind of optimism about the future was one of the key factors in Job's change of mind. He writes:

> God made it clear that he had not been totally defeated by the events of the past but was still capable of giving meaning to life. In other words, apart from all appearances, Job still had a future in God, for God had a future in Job. . . .
>
> No one ever moves out of the shadows of grief apart from some form of this hope.[6]

Myron Madden correctly states a similar principle:

> The essence of despair is relegating God solely to the past. And what is nostalgia if it is not the fear that God cannot do as well in the future as he has done in the past?[7]

After a serious illness, some people prefer to remain invalids rather than go through the discipline of convalescence. The same is true with the immediate or anticipated loss of a spouse through death or divorce. The following description of the loss David Bogard felt after his wife's death could be applied to the situation of a nearly divorced person:

> He [the remaining spouse] is somewhat like a person whose leg has been amputated, for a part of him is gone. He must now learn to walk again, alone; unless he is willing to remain a mental and spiritual invalid the rest of his life.[8]

That's where you are right now. You hurt. Divorce is imminent. Is life going to go on for you, or are you going to choose to be an emotional and spiritual cripple the rest of your life?

THE EFFECTS OF CHANGE

If you've really been working on your mental attitude and planning for the future, then you should be open to accepting the fact that your marriage is almost over. You have probably listed the things that you want in your divorce settlement and have given some thought to the future. You must also prepare yourself for the changes divorce will bring. If you are like most people, you are a creature of habit and find a great deal of security in doing things the same way every day. One of the emotionally disturbing elements of divorce is a break with the familiar routine. But don't be afraid. This break may offer you exciting new possibilities.

Your divorce, for example, may lead to a new routine of employment. If you are a woman, you may have to begin work and arrange to have your children cared for while you're working. Rather than lament the fact that you must work, look at your job as an exciting opportunity to expand your mind and your contacts with other people in a way that you never could when you were married and not working. When you begin to feel uncomfortable and annoyed with the changes of routine, realize that the discomfort will pass when you adjust to them.

Resist the temptation to dump your annoyance, yes, even anger, on your former spouse. Many divorced people go around the rest of their lives angry and bitter, missing the good they could carve out of a new life because they refuse to get rid of this emotional poison. Again, say aloud, "This is a new day, and I can make it a great day. I'm going to look for opportunities to change what I can, in order to make it an even greater day. I will not let circumstances control me; with God's help, I will control them. And once I have discharged my responsibility to make something of my life, I will let God take care of what I cannot change." Realize that your anger is really precipitated by *change* and not by your former spouse. Yes, your former spouse was partially responsible for that change, but it's the *change* that's angering you. If you spent as much energy dealing with the problems of change as you do with being angry at your former spouse, you would master the new routine a lot sooner.

I think of Dan, who sat in my office last year and sobbed, "I can't live without her." He then shared how Karen, his wife, had left him, primarily because she claimed that he was too demanding. Even in our conversations, when he tried to figure out how to be less dominating, he dominated. "I'll let her do whatever she wants to do," he often said. "I'll buy her whatever she wants. I'll fix the house however she likes it. I'll even buy her a new house." Even in the midst of his pain, Dan had to do all the fixing of the relationship. Unable to approach the marriage any other way, he couldn't understand why his wife considered him so demanding.

As I listened, I understood why Karen had left him. Trapped and smothered, she felt like the proverbial bird in a gilded cage. She had everything money could buy, but she still felt trapped. Why? Because Dan had to do the fixing. He couldn't let her go, but he couldn't let her feel free.

When Karen finally divorced him and got custody of the children, Dan was crushed. Usually very successful in his work, he now floundered. He spent hours just sitting and staring at the wall in his office. I don't doubt that he loved Karen and missed her deeply. But there was another aspect of his situation that he was not facing—the psychological impact of losing control and having a change forced on him that he could do nothing about. He had controlled almost every circumstance he had encountered, either through power and money or by dismissing it as something trivial. But now, for the first time in his life, Dan had no control over something desperately important to him. Someone else was dictating the terms of change in his life, and he didn't know how to handle it.

Until he was willing to recognize the psychological impact of a change beyond his control, he stuck to his point. "What can I do to get Karen back?" he would repeat, rather than accepting the change and making a new life.

NEW TASKS, NEW FRUSTRATIONS, NEW GROWTH

You will find it difficult at first to do what appear to be simple tasks. For the man who has never cooked, preparing meals may seem beyond his abilities. What aggravates matters further is that he knows that cooking is something he can do if he has to, but he finds it so difficult. Why? Again, he may be resisting change. He may not say it aloud, but he may think, *Why must I do this when I've never had to before?*

To adjust to a new task, you should take pride in accomplishing it, no matter how ridiculously simple it seems to be. If you can't take pride in the meal itself, for example, take pride in the fact that you prepared it. By doing so, you are demonstrating to yourself your willingness to accept change. And that's the victory.

The same sense of victory applies to the woman who takes her car to be serviced for the first time. By accomplishing that task—talking to the mechanic, getting an estimate, picking the car up afterward—she has said, *By that act, I am willing to accept the reality that my marriage is over. I accept the responsibility for new tasks.*

The accomplishment of a new task will not only put the reality of the dead marriage in proper perspective, but also give you a sense of security. You will start believing that maybe you can make it in life without the spouse you depended on to do certain tasks. Take pride in the new tasks you accomplish, no matter how small, because *you* have done them.

Another adjustment you must make is the way you relate to your children. A mother will not have nearly so much time for her children as she once did, primarily because she will probably have a job in addition to everything else entailed in being a mother and homemaker. She may become bitter toward her ex-husband for putting all these demands on her. But is she going to spend her energy mentally blasting her husband, or is she going to spend it getting busy about the task of solo parenting and using it as an opportunity to make a new and exciting life for herself?

If you settle into a dull, dead routine and don't cultivate outside interests, you will have a hard time adjusting, no matter how light the demands made on you. Now that you have an opportunity to spend your time the way *you* want to, make the most of it. Mel Krantzler writes:

> In the first painful weeks of separation, free time is the last thing most people want. I can still recall my dread of the empty evening hours during the first weeks of my separation. Yet, comforting as a daily routine may appear in retrospect, consider the price one has paid for that security. The most desolate man and woman can usually point to at least one example of welcome free time, even in the initial stages of divorce. As an older woman whose husband had left her confessed, "We always had to have dinner at 6:15 on the dot. The house had to be spotless;

if he found dust on the window sill, he would write 'dirty' in it. I still miss him, but I must admit it's a relief not to have to dust all day. And now I can eat when *I* feel like it.". . .

One man whose wife had insisted he spend every evening and weekend hour on household improvements and yard work found that, while the pain of initial separation was severe, it was somewhat alleviated by not having to don old clothes after a day at the office and edge the front walk. "I never really liked doing that stuff," he said. "Now I find out I'm really an apartment dweller at heart. I have no qualms about leaving the joys of fixing the faucet to the superintendent while I relax with a good book." . . .

When your children are visiting your spouse, use that time to explore your new independence. You may not want to take (or be able to afford) a cruise or trip abroad, but you can savor the freedom of eating *when* you want, *what* you want and watching *your* favorite T.V. program or sleeping lage undisturbed. . . .

Each departure from your established routine, however small, is proof of your ability to face—and even enjoy—the facts of single life.[9]

CHAPTER 3

What You Need to Know About Divorce Laws

Divorce is first and foremost a lawsuit. One spouse must bring suit against the other spouse in an adversary proceeding authorized by a court of law. Christians and others with religious sensitivity and conviction who are caught up in divorce may find such a prospect disagreeable. Nevertheless, if you are the unwilling party to a divorce, it is perfectly proper from a biblical perspective to defend yourself. What's more, if you and your spouse agree to separate, you are not dragging a believer into court against his will (as discussed in 1 Corinthians 6:1-8).

The purpose of this chapter is not to dispense legal advice. If you need advice, hire a lawyer. Friends who have had satisfactory dealings with lawyers are often a good referral source. Your local Bar Association is another good source. Libraries usually have a copy of Martindale-Hubbell's *Law Directory*, which will provide information on lawyers' education, specialty, experience, assets, and even ratings on competence.

An extremely helpful book is titled *How to Get a Divorce.*[1] Although this book was written for residents of the District of Columbia, Maryland, and Virginia, it contains much general information on divorce. It includes an appendix that gives grounds for divorce and residency requirements for all fifty states, the District of Columbia, Puerto Rico, and the Virgin Islands.

COMMON QUESTIONS ABOUT DIVORCE PROCEEDINGS

How Do I Select a Lawyer?

Choose one who is competent, interested in your case, and returns your phone calls. He should be made aware of your religious convictions and be able to understand how they might affect the case. Your attorney should not feel hamstrung, nor should you put yourself in the position of having to compromise your convictions. You and your attorney must be able to work together effectively.

What Will an Attorney Cost?

Usually an attorney will require a nonrefundable retainer fee from as low as $250 to as high as $2,500. The fee is based on the complexity of the case. In a hotly contested divorce, the fees could run as high as $10,000. An article in the February 10, 1975, issue of *Business Week* reported that inflation has sent the total cost of divorce soaring, usually a minimum of $1,500 per partner in legal fees alone.[2] You and your attorney should negotiate the fee you are required to pay.

If you do retain an attorney, make sure that you understand what his fees are and when they are to be paid—and pay them promptly. An attorney, like other professionals, depends on recompense for his services for his bread and butter. You will be sure to receive the very best service he can offer if you pay promptly.

Can I Legally Be My Own Lawyer?

You have the right to represent yourself unless the presiding judge rules otherwise. Such a proceeding is called *pro se*. In an amiable settlement that involves only a little property, acting as your own lawyer might be to your advantage. But you will find that the complexities of the law will test your patience.

In most cases, an attorney's advice is well worth his fee. If you do not wish to retain an attorney to handle your case, you might obtain his advice for a fee, which not uncommonly starts at $50 an hour.

One of the big advantages in using an attorney is that he knows everything that should be included in the divorce settlement. If he is an expert on divorce law, he will also be able to give you some pointers on how to take the best tax advantages.

Do the Spouses Need Separate Lawyers?

If your spouse is divorcing you, his attorney will be representing his interests, which include any financial or property settlements. If the circumstances of the divorce are nasty, then you certainly will want an attorney to represent your interests. He will recognize a reasonable settlement and will know what your spouse's attorney and the court are likely to consider reasonable terms.

If you and your spouse can agree to terms of settlement beforehand, an attorney can represent both of you. If, however, you decide later that you're going to fight it out in court, your attorney can't ethically represent both of you. One of you must then seek another attorney.

Grounds for Divorce

A general guide for grounds for divorce is shown in figure 1. Remember that divorce laws are constantly changing. "No-fault" divorce, which permits either party to get a divorce without having to show grounds, is becoming increasingly popular. As of 1975, every state except Illinois, Massachusetts, Mississippi, Pennsylvania, and South Dakota had some type of no-fault laws.[3]

In the District of Columbia, Maryland, and Virginia, voluntary separation from bed and board without cohabitation is a ground for divorce. This usually means that you and your spouse have separated after mutually and voluntarily agreeing that you no longer wish to live together as husband and wife and that there's no hope of reconciliation. Even if you don't want a separation, your spouse can still file under the ground

WHAT THE DIVORCE LAWS SAY COAST TO COAST

	GROUNDS FOR DIVORCE					DIVISION OF PROPERTY			ALIMONY		
	BREAKDOWN OF MARRIAGE	STANDARD FAULT GROUNDS	INCOMPATIBILITY	SEPARATION	ALCOHOLISM OR DRUG USE	COURT CANNOT MAKE A DISTRIBUTION	COURT EMPOWERED TO DISTRIBUTE	COMMUNITY PROPERTY—JOINT OWNERSHIP	TO EITHER SPOUSE	TO WIFE ONLY	NO ALIMONY
Alabama	●	●		●	●	●				●	
Alaska		●	●		●		●		●		
Arizona	●							●	●		
Arkansas		●		●	●		●			●	
California	●						●	●	●		
Colorado	●						●		●		
Connecticut	●	●		●	●		●		●		
Delaware	●						●		●		
Dist. of Columbia		●		●			●		●		
Florida	●					●			●		
Georgia	●	●			●	●			●		
Hawaii	●	●				●			●		
Idaho	●	●	●					●	●		
Illinois		●			●		●		●		
Indiana	●	●					●		●		
Iowa	●						●		●		
Kansas		●	●		●		●		●		
Kentucky	●						●		●		
Louisiana		●		●	●			●			●*
Maine	●	●					●		●		
Maryland		●		●		●				●	
Massachusetts		●			●	●			●		
Michigan	●						●		●		
Minnesota	●						●		●		
Mississippi		●			●	●				●	
Missouri	●						●		●		
Montana	●	●					●		●		
Nebraska	●						●		●		
Nevada		●	●		●			●	●		
New Hampshire	●	●		●	●		●		●**		
New Jersey	●			●			●		●		
New Mexico		●	●					●	●		
New York		●		●		●			●		
North Carolina		●		●		●					●***
North Dakota		●	●		●		●		●		
Ohio		●		●	●	●			●		
Oklahoma		●	●		●		●		●		
Oregon	●						●		●		
Pennsylvania		●				●					●
Rhode Island		●		●	●	●				●	
South Carolina		●		●	●	●				●	
South Dakota		●			●		●			●	
Tennessee		●		●	●		●			●	
Texas		●		●				●			●
Utah		●		●	●		●		●		
Vermont		●		●			●		●		
Virginia		●		●		●			●		
Washington	●							●	●		
West Virginia		●		●	●		●		●		
Wisconsin		●		●	●		●			●	
Wyoming		●		●	●		●		●		

Notes: Standard fault grounds include adultery, cruelty, desertion. Separation means living apart with normal financial support provided. In division of property, when court cannot make a distribution, property goes to husband or wife, depending on who has legal title.

*Louisiana limits alimony to ½ of the husband's income

**New Hampshire limits alimony to a term of three years (subject to renewal)

***North Carolina provides for alimony only if the spouse is unable to work cited above, though the waiting period for the final divorce decree is longer. It's not absolutely necessary in all states to live under separate roofs under a voluntary separation agreement. In any case, the separation must be continuous, and any sexual relations with your spouse will void the agreement.

Most lawyers prefer to accept voluntary separation cases, mainly because in a case of this type, it's easy to prove the ground for divorce. Generally all that's needed are the testimonies of the plaintiff and the plaintiff's witness that separation has actually occurred. Also, in a voluntary separation case, no guilt need be proved and no dirty laundry is aired in court. This is an important consideration, since divorce proceedings are a matter of public record and can be read by anyone whenever the court clerk's office is open.

Of course, you can file for divorce on other grounds allowed by your state. Remember, however, that divorce is a lawsuit. One spouse is charging the other in an adversary proceeding: there is no such thing as a "nice divorce." It is possible to make it difficult for your spouse to divorce you. The law does require acceptable grounds for divorce. But if your spouse is determined to divorce you, you will gain little by blocking it. Such an attempt will tend only to harden the divorcing spouse and make the divorce proceedings even nastier. When children are involved, blocking the divorce perpetuates the strain between the parents and produces far more trauma for the children than the actual divorce and parting of ways.

I don't mean to imply that I favor no-fault divorce laws unreservedly. The economic well-being of a dependent spouse and children should not be sacrificed for an amiable settlement. Divorces shouldn't be made any nastier than they have to be, but be sure that the settlement is fair, especially for the dependent party to the divorce.

No-fault divorce may also make some couples think that divorce is an easy way out of a painful relationship. They may not consider the financial and emotional hardships that divorce can inflict—hardships that may be greater than the efforts needed to make the marriage work. Donald Schiller, a Chicago attorney, made the following comments on no-fault divorce laws while he was vice chairman of the American Bar Association's committee on divorce law:

> Individuals now take divorce as an easy solution to marital problems. Many people divorce before giving a potentially good marriage a chance, and many people divorce without looking at their personal problems that could be solved by counseling—so they are back in court for second and third divorces without learning anything.[4]

What Is Alimony?

Alimony, now usually referred to as "support and maintenance," is payable by either spouse in twenty-eight states, depending on who is the breadwinner.[5] Currently the trend of the courts is to award less alimony, and the frequency of cases in which it is awarded is also decreasing. In 1976, for example, alimony was awarded in only 15 percent of all divorce cases.[6] In cases where each spouse has an income and compensation is being made for property division, a lump sum may be paid in lieu of alimony.

Usually the husband will pay alimony until the wife remarries, but will almost never pay more than 50 percent of his net income. Even when children are involved, alimony may be as low as 30 percent, and when no children are involved, alimony may be as low as 20 percent. A young woman who can work may be told by the court that she will have to help out by going to work.

In negotiating a settlement, remember that the days are over when a wife can expect very comfortable terms. One attorney who handles more than twenty-five divorce cases a year said, "If I represent the wife, I look upon the result as good if she ends up with 10 to 15 percent of her husband's take-home money."[7]

When the final terms of the separation agreement are laid out, make sure that they include any possible modification of alimony due to inflationary pressure, job loss, or sickness on the part of the person paying alimony. Also, be careful about the terms under which you waive alimony. If you need it later and have received nothing in the agreement, you'll be out of luck. The best course to follow is to consult a competent attorney, who can assist you in planning the terms of alimony that should be included in the separation agreement.

How Much Alimony Should I Ask For?

To deal with alimony, begin by figuring out how much you spend on food, rent or house payments, furnishings, clothing, utilities, automobile (including gas, repairs, and insurance), insurance premiums (life, health, and homeowner's insurance), medical care, and entertainment. You should also figure 5 percent of the total for yearly inflation. It is not unreasonable to add another 5 to 10 percent for savings. Your guideline should be reasonableness. It won't do you or anyone else any good to try to "get even" financially.

One last principle to remember is that you may find it difficult to get over your unwanted divorce if you have to see your former spouse every time he drops the money by the house. Former husbands who insist on delivering the alimony payments personally make things tough on former wives who are having a hard time adjusting to their single life. Directing your lawyer to spell out terms in the agreement that will keep you and your former spouse apart might be beneficial. For example, the support checks could be mailed to you.

The Property Settlement

In addition to alimony, the separation agreement—also known as the property settlement—must be considered. This agreement spells out what you will receive upon separation and what you most likely will receive when the divorce is final. Although the settlement may be amended later through further litigation, it has the force of a legally binding contract.

The agreement includes alimony, custody of children, child support, ownership of motor vehicles, division of such personal property as jewelry and the family dog, division of real property (such as the family home or your weekend retreat), medical expenses for the dependent spouse and/or children, whether joint tax returns are to be filed, how charge accounts and credit are to be handled, terms of payment of outstanding bills, provision for life insurance in the event of the death of the spouse providing alimony and/or child support, division of jointly held stocks or bonds, division of any checking or savings accounts, rights to visit the children, and any other matters that are in your best interest to put in writing.

The time you and your spouse spend formulating the specific terms of the settlement won't be easy emotionally. Once you start putting down on paper who gets what, the reality of the breakup will hit you again. Be careful that you don't become so emotionally overwrought that you can't even begin to think in terms of a fair settlement. Unable to think of divorce, much less of a settlement, a spouse will often spend this time crying and lashing out instead of negotiating the settlement. But tears and anger won't change things. Even if the settlement is delayed out of spite, it will come about in time.

You should give some thought to what a fair settlement might be. The most basic principle to remember is that both you and your spouse must be willing to bargain. Division of property acquired during marriage usually follows a fifty-fifty formula. In most cases, the wife gets the house; this is almost the rule if children are involved. If a great deal of property is involved, be careful that you don't incur a big tax bill by transferring appreciated property. The fees you will pay a good attorney and accountant will be well spent when they use their skills to help you avoid additional financial hardship. If you try to be hard-nosed, both of you may be the losers; you may escalate your attorney's fees and still not get any more than was originally offered. It won't do any good to try to use the settlement to get even, because the court won't hear outrageous demands. The more reasonable you can be in the negotiations, the easier you will make it on yourself emotionally.

Emotions can and usually do get in the way of achieving a satisfactory settlement. Ann Diamond, a California divorce lawyer, lists seven emotion-packed situations that inhibit a fair settlement:

- A rejected spouse, unable to accept the finality of the separation, may agree to almost any demand of the other party in the hope that it will facilitate a reconciliation.

- A woman accustomed to having her husband make all important decisions will continue to look to him for advice, even though he has left her and is no longer interested in protecting her.
- The long-suffering, passive mate often seeks redress in the settlement for all past miseries of the relationship, whether self-inflicted or otherwise.
- When the break-up is sudden, the rejected spouse may be so traumatized that he, or more frequently she, is unable to make any realistic estimate of future financial need.
- The spouse who wants out may feel so guilty that he or she will try to compensate by being overly generous in property division and agree to pay or receive support payments which are too high or too low. The subsequent resentment which can erupt in the long run will only cause further problems for both.
- Because the rejected partner may be too depressed to face any additional pressure, he or she will consent to any financial settlement just to get matters over with.
- One spouse may use the children as a means to punish and get even with the rejecting partner.[8]

Yes, drafting a settlement can arouse deep anger and resentment, but you don't do yourself a favor when you indulge in them. After you cool off, you may have saddled yourself with a settlement that will be unsatisfactory for years just because you indulged at settlement time.

Divorce and Custody Suits

"The parents, divorced or divorcing, who take unresolved problems concerning their children to court in search of a wise solution will rarely find it there," according to Dr. Louise Despert.[9] Not only will the parents be disappointed by a court-imposed decision, but they will also find that custody granted by a court is almost never permanent. By virtue of the fact that a custody suit was "lost" in court and terms were imposed by the court, the "winning" parent can almost guarantee that he will be in court again on the matter. Only one possible agreement can give the child any assurance that he

/ 37

will not be a legal pawn: the parents must mutually agree on what is in *his best interest*. This decision may be determined outside the court, with the help of parties sympathetic to and conversant with the child's needs.

At the end of this chapter I have listed some agencies that offer a husband and wife guidance on the matter of their child's custody. In addition to contacting one of these agencies, Christian parents will also want to check with a pastor concerning Christian counselors or agencies in their locale. The pastor will provide what help he can in determining the best course for the child, and if he feels that the problem is beyond his expertise, he will be able to suggest Christian counselors who can help. Even if one of the parents is unwilling to get a counselor's viewpoint on what is best for the child, the other parent would do well to get a counselor's viewpoint before getting involved in a custody suit. But each parent must ask himself, *Do I honestly want what is best for my child, or do I want what is best for me?*

Child Support

While you are deciding what kind of settlement would be fair to you, you might also begin thinking about child support payments. These payments vary greatly. Such factors as living standard, type of schooling, and the wife's ability to work will be taken into consideration. The resulting payments are based on the child's *reasonable* needs. A divorce action is an equity action in which the judge acts as both judge and jury; common sense prevails.

In figuring child support, determine how much you pay for clothing, food, doctors, dentists, incidentals such as Girl Scout uniforms and Little League equipment, and special costs such as school field trips, camps, and private lessons. You should also determine how and when the payments will be made and what action will be taken when payment is not made. Sometimes a block of stock or a piece of real estate is held in escrow by the attorney as a safeguard.

Help is available to those whose spouses skip town and don't pay. Federal legislation took effect in January 1977 that requires the Department of Health, Education, and Welfare to set up a Parent Locator Service. Once caught, the errant spouse will have to appear in court and explain his reasons for nonsupport.

Don't neglect to consider tax advantages when considering child support. Child support is not tax deductible, but alimony is. By increasing your alimony and reducing child support, more of the husband's payment is tax deductible. The wife will have to pay taxes on the increased alimony, but because of his tax deductible advantage, the husband may be able to give her more money. The result is a net increase for the wife, because Uncle Sam is taking out a smaller chunk.

Child Visitation

The final consideration is the kind of child visitation you and your spouse will choose. Begin by defining the noncustodial parent's terms of visitation clearly. Often the terms are vaguely defined as "reasonable and proper," which leaves the definition up to the parents. Usually one day a week and two weekends a month are considered reasonable.

Since it is emotionally difficult to get over an unwanted divorce when you see your former spouse regularly, figure out ways in which the visitation of the children will allow you to avoid contact with your spouse altogether.

Divorce courts attempt to be equitable. But no matter how equitable they attempt to be, the divorce will probably be a financial hardship on both spouses. Unless you are wealthy, expect to settle for a lower standard of living. The harsh economic reality is that it costs more to support two households than one.

It should go without saying that divorce proceedings should not be fixed without careful thought to the financial as well as emotional costs. Yet many couples are surprised at what a divorce really costs. Unfortunately, by the time they get into a divorce, they are so emotionally committed to the idea that they find it difficult to back off and renew their relationship.

Agencies for Custody Counseling

The Family Service Association of America, 192 Lexington Avenue, New York, N. Y. 10016 (for family agencies).

The Child Welfare League, Inc., 24 West 40th Street, New York, N. Y. 10018 (for child guidance agencies).

The National Association for Mental Health, Inc., 1790 Broadway, New York, N. Y. 10019 (for psychiatric clinics or qualified psychiatrists).

The American Association of Marriage and Family Counselors, 225 Yale Ave., Claremont, Ca. 71711 (for family agencies).

The National Association of Social Workers, 1425 H St., N. W., Suite 600, Washington, D. C. 20005 (for family agencies).

CHAPTER 4

Biblical Teaching on Divorce

With divorces in the United States totaling a million a year and desertions running close to another million, it's inevitable that many Christians will be swept up in the whirlwind.[1] As divorces increase among faithful Christians and their children, and as more divorced people seek church membership, the church is being pressed to take a less rigid stand on divorce.

I'm treating the question of divorce separately from that of remarriage for both practical and theological reasons. People who don't want a divorce or who divorce reluctantly usually don't have remarriage in mind, at least not immediately. The practical issue they face is that of divorce—its theological and practical consequences. For the Christian who is the unwilling victim of divorce or who feels that he must end a marriage out of necessity, the question of divorce as a sin enters the picture.

Is divorce in and of itself a sin? Or, to put it another way, if a Christian divorces and does not remarry, does he sin? And if it can be determined that he is sinning, what then? Is he faced with the dilemma of remaining in a marriage that is destroying him emotionally and physically or else bearing the stigma of an adulterer?

Rather than take a dogmatic stand on divorce, I wish to examine the divorce dilemma from the following perspectives. The first perspective is to separate the divorce issue from remarriage and ask whether or not divorce in and of itself is sin. The other perspective, which we will examine in the chapter on remarriage, is based on what is called "a redemptive attitude." The redemptive attitude says, "Yes, divorce is a sin. But it's a sin that can be forgiven like any other sin. It should not forever exclude believers from fellowship with God and the church."

The Christian facing divorce is the one who ultimately must decide where he stands before God as a divorced person. However, this does not mean that the church must avoid taking a stand on divorce. Rather, the church has an increasing responsibility to teach the Word of God and apply it to the question of divorce. Practically speaking, the church has not taken the lead in this matter; believers have decided what they are going to do with or without the church's blessing—and they will probably continue to do so.

When speakers and writers broach the subject of divorce, they usually trace the following biblical truths taught by Moses, Jesus, and Paul.

MOSES' TEACHING ON DIVORCE

Moses' central teaching on divorce is recorded in Deuteronomy 24.

> When a man takes a wife and marries her, and it happens that she finds no favor in his eyes because he has found some indecency in her, and he writes her a certificate of divorce and puts it in her hand and sends her out from his house, and she leaves his house and goes and becomes another man's wife, and if the latter husband turns against her and writes her a certificate of divorce and puts it in her hand and sends her out of his house, or if the latter husband dies who took her to be his wife, then her former husband who sent her away is not allowed to take her again to be his wife, since she has been defiled; for that is an abomination before the Lord, and you shall not bring sin on the land which the Lord your God gives you as an inheritance.[2]

According to this passage, God permitted divorce on the ground of "indecency." Some people have taught that indecency is marital infidelity. Others have argued that this could not be the meaning, since the law stated that an adulterer must be stoned,[3] and the woman in this passage was set free to go her own way and remarry. They then interpret the passage to mean that a man in the Jewish culture could divorce his wife at the slightest displeasure.

Even in Jesus' day, the Jews disagreed over the interpretation of Deuteronomy 24, and two distinct schools of thought emerged on divorce. One, the liberal school of Hillel, granted divorce for any cause; the other, the conservative school of Shammai, permitted divorce only on the ground of infidelity.[4] Regardless of the interpretations, however, the law of Moses—which was declared to be holy, just, and good—provided for divorce.

JESUS' TEACHING ON DIVORCE

Jesus recognized the provision for divorce in the law of Moses. But He made it clear that God did not establish the pattern of divorce at Creation. God only granted it, Jesus said, because of mankind's "hardness of heart."[5] The entrance of sin into the world prompted God to act graciously toward sinful men, whose sinfulness was demonstrated by their inability to live with their wives.

In the context of the Jews' disagreement over divorce, Jesus addressed His teachings on divorce to those who would follow Him. These messages are recorded in Matthew 5:32; 19:3-12; Mark 10:11-12; and Luke 16:18. Jesus proposed that by His grace, His followers would be able to do what they couldn't do under the law—live together without the necessity of divorce. This, He taught, is the ideal that Christians should strive to attain.

Except for one occasion, whenever Jesus spoke of divorce, He spoke also of remarriage. With one exception, Jesus labeled divorce *and* remarriage adultery. But is divorce by itself a sin? This question is especially relevant today, because a person can be divorced even if he doesn't want to be.

The single passage in which Jesus speaks of divorce by itself is Matthew 5:32. There He says, "But I say to you that every one who divorces his wife, except for the cause of unchastity, makes her commit adultery; and whoever marries a divorced woman commits adultery." Some expositors interpret this passage to mean that the very act of divorcing a woman makes her an adulteress. Others, on the other hand, say that she is an adulteress only in that she is expected to remarry.

In its article on marriage, the *International Standard Bible Encyclopedia (ISBE)* records, "Divorce to a Jew carried with it the right of remarriage, and the words 'causeth her to commit adultery' (Matt. 5:32) show that Jesus assumed that the divorced woman would marry again."[6]

D. Martyn Lloyd-Jones takes the same position. "Therefore, if you put away your wife for any other reason you are putting her away without breaking the bond. In this way you are making her break the bond if she should marry again; and she is therefore committing adultery."[7]

If *ISBE* and Dr. Lloyd-Jones are correct, it would seem, then, that the stigma of adultery can be avoided if a Christian divorces but does not remarry. The apostle Paul bears this out in his teaching on divorce.

PAUL'S TEACHING ON DIVORCE

Speaking to Corinthian women who had divorced their husbands, Paul added further perspective to the subject of divorce between Christians. The following verses, addressed to a Gentile church exposed to a sexually permissive society, are applicable to Christians living in Western society today. Paul was definitely referring to divorce between Christians in this passage, since the verses following this quotation specifically address the subject of a believer's marriage to an unbeliever.

> But to the married I give instructions, not I, but the Lord, that the wife should not leave her husband (but if she does leave, let her remain unmarried, or else be reconciled to her husband), and that the husband should not send his wife away.[8]

Paul recalled in these words what Jesus had said in the Gospels. A wife should not "leave" her husband. The word *leave,* translated from the Greek word *koridzetai,* means "divorce." The meaning is clear within the context of this passage, for if the woman were still married to the husband she left, Paul would not have told her to remain unmarried. Rather, he would have said, "Leave, but remain *married."* Based on these teachings, the Corinthian women who had divorced their husbands were not violating the principles Jesus laid down on divorce as long as they either remained unmarried or were reconciled to their husbands.

The principle we must recognize here is that Paul did not say to the Corinthian Christians, "It doesn't matter how impossible your marital situation is. If you divorce, you have sinned." This does not mean that Paul held a low view of marriage. Indeed, his other writings reflect a very high view. But in the above passage, he showed us how Jesus' words are to be applied to an absolutely intolerable marriage.

Some expositors argue that Paul is not giving the Corinthians guidance for future marital conflicts. Instead, they hold that the passage offers guidance in cases where such conflicts have already occurred. Others disagree. Godet, for example, points out that the Corinthians were divorcing *in spite of* Jesus' statement of the ideal, a situation that still occurs today:

> Paul could perfectly anticipate the case in which, notwithstanding this prohibition, a wife, outraged by the bad treatment of which she was the victim, would go off abruptly in a moment of lively irritation. Fearing to do more harm than good by doing violence to the state of things, Paul accepts the situation. But first he seeks to prevent a second and still graver evil from being added to the first, and that by a new marriage of the separated wife, a marriage which Jesus called adultery; then he recommends a reconciliation as soon as possible.[9]

H. A. W. Meyer, supporting Godet's view, maintains that Paul was not addressing those who had already separated. Meyer believes that the separation discussed here is "an occurrence which will possibly be realized in the experience of the future."[10]

This approach to divorce is quite contrary to the counsel traditionally given to a person under such circumstances. Usually the stigma of adultery is raised whenever a Christian talks about divorcing a Christian spouse. The Christian is then put in a position of having to choose between an intolerable marriage that may be ruining him physically and emotionally or wearing the stigmatic label "adulterer."

The apostle Paul took the subject of adultery very seriously. Certainly he wasn't saying that adultery was proper. If the woman in 1 Corinthians 7:10-11 was committing adultery by divorcing her husband, Paul would have established a rationale similar to the biblical rationale on the subject of killing: To kill someone by an act of murder, for example, is a sin; but to kill as an act of execution or in a just war is not a sin. Likewise, divorce without remarriage is not adultery. The divorced woman described in Matthew 5:32 will probably remarry and, for this reason, the husband makes her an adulteress. But she is not an adulteress if she does not remarry.

Paul separates divorce and remarriage to meet a very practical problem. What are the options for a Christian woman who is caught in an impossible marriage to a professing Christian husband? She is given permission to divorce, with the provision that she either remain unmarried or be reconciled to her husband. Divorce without remarriage is not an adulterous act.

Many people react strongly when I express this point of view. "Two Christian people," they immediately say, "ought to be able to settle their differences." Certainly this is the ideal that Christ calls us to attain. But the fact remains that we often don't live up to that ideal any more than other biblical ideals.

Paul and Barnabas are a good example. If ever two godly men should have been able to settle their differences, they should have. Yet the Bible records a serious disagreement between them. Evidently John Mark had fallen short of Paul's expectations on the previous missionary journey, and Paul didn't want him along on the second trip. Barnabas, John Mark's uncle, wanted to take him along. Their *sharp* disagreement led to a parting of ways (see Acts 15:36-41).

You may say, "But Paul and Barnabas weren't married. Their situation had nothing to do with marital separation or divorce." True enough. But it was the disagreement and separation of two godly men. What happens, then, to the common argument that two Christians ought to be able to settle their differences? That kind of give-and-take relationship is ideal, both in and out of marriage. But the formulation of that ideal doesn't mean that we will always live up to it. As God's people, we are sinners saved by grace. As such, we will not always live up to God's ideals. And God, knowing our weaknesses, makes provision for our failures. He either provides us with an alternative course of action or forgives our sin when there is no alternative to what He commands.

Paul describes in 1 Corinthians 7 what a believer should do if his marriage to an unbeliever becomes intolerable:

> But to the rest I say, not the Lord, that if any brother has a wife who is an unbeliever, and she consents to live with him, let him not send her away. And a woman who has an unbelieving husband, and he consents to live with her, let her not send her husband away. For the unbelieving husband is sanctified through his wife, and the unbelieving wife is sanctified through her believing husband; for otherwise your children are unclean, but now they are holy. Yet if the unbelieving one leaves, let him leave.[11]

Once again, the ideal situation is to keep the marriage intact and not to divorce the unbeliever. The purpose of keeping the marriage intact is to expose the unbeliever to the believer's witness. However, if the unbeliever does not want to keep the marriage intact, that's another matter. The unbeliever may express this verbally or through his behavior. The word *consent* in verses 12-13 actually means "to be pleased with" or "content with." A man with gross, intolerable behavior certainly is not pleased with or content with his marriage. State laws call such intolerable behavior "constructive desertion." The intolerable person in question may not leave, but he forces the spouse to leave. Like the woman with the Christian husband, the woman in this situation has the right to divorce her spouse and either remain unmarried or be reconciled to him in the future.

Summing Up the Biblical Perspective

I'm not suggesting by all this that divorce is good. It is less than

God's ideal and must be recognized as such. But seeing divorce in this perspective will keep us from being indifferent about preserving a marriage and will also help us avoid being trapped in a relationship.

Dr. Allen Verhey, writing in the *Reformed Journal*, expresses the same point in reference to Jesus' teaching on divorce.

> The saying on divorce is a part of Jesus's teaching. He is not giving some counsel of perfection. He is not describing some "interims-ethik" not applicable if the end of the world is no longer thought imminent. He is not giving *halakah* or a simple moral rule strictly applicable to external behavior. He is not proposing an "impossible ideal" to drive us to hope in the gospel. He is announcing the gospel, the kingdom, and he is forming the dispositions and character which are appropriate to the gospel, to the fulfillment of God's intentions with his creation. The command, then, is to be understood not as a moral rule but as an invitation or a permission to share in the freedom Jesus gives to live marriage as God intended and intends.[12]

THE REDEMPTIVE APPROACH

Another way of approaching the divorce dilemma is with what is called "a redemptive approach." Stanley A. Ellisen makes a powerful plea for this approach in his book *Divorce and Remarriage in the Church.*

> Another caution should be observed in approaching the problem. That is to studiously avoid a spirit of self-righteousness and judgment. Only he who is without sin should cast stones or judgmental glances. Jesus alone had this qualification, and yet His attitude toward sinners of every stripe was that of compassion and discipline. Our attitude must be a reflection of His if our service is to be effective.[13]

He goes on to show that God Himself was involved in a divorce suit with Israel.

> This court action He states in Hosea 2 and proceeds to elaborate throughout the book. His wail in Hosea 11:8 summarizes His feeling toward the nation and dramatically reflects the sobs of many bereft partners as He exclaims, "How shall I give thee up, Ephraim?" God Himself had to get a divorce because of His beloved's unfaithfulness.[14]

If God is a compassionate Friend rather than a censorious Judge, then the church and individual Christians should follow His example. Let no one suppose that this is a "soft" approach to divorce. My experience with Christians involved in divorce has shown me that most are exceedingly reluctant to divorce and don't abuse the redemptive attitude Ellisen writes about. They are either unwilling victims of a spouse's divorce action or file for divorce only after physical or emotional trauma.

Wanda is a good example of the reluctance many Christians have when they are faced with the possibility of divorce. She was suffering from a severe case of colitis when her doctor finally found out what was bothering her. Her husband, a professing Christian, was cruel and abusive. And even though Wanda didn't talk back, her body did. She told her doctor that she couldn't leave her husband because she was a Christian; she felt it was her duty to stay with him. The doctor responded that if she didn't leave him, she'd wind up in the hospital—and then he sent her to me hoping that I could do something to change her mind.

When I asked her why she would not consider leaving her husband, Wanda gave me the same response. "As a Christian, I can't leave him," she said, wiping tears away with her sleeve. "Even though he abuses me a lot, he has never been unfaithful and supports me and the children." She refused to change her attitude even after both her children began to show signs of emotional disturbance and she finally wound up in the hospital, where doctors removed all of her large intestine.

Wanda, now physically handicapped, is having difficulty adjusting to her limitations. And she still refuses to divorce her husband. Her decision may seem like remarkable heroism— but it really isn't. She is so dependent on her husband that she prefers a bad marriage to being alone. If she could get herself together and file for divorce, many would accept that as the best course to follow. Certainly the redemptive attitude should be applied in this situation.

Ellisen further emphasizes the need to apply the redemptive attitude when he writes:

/ 49

We often forget how intimate His compassion is toward those with marital problems. His concern is a very knowing sympathy, born of experience, not a condescending, judgmental censure. He has personally suffered the same tragedy. No wonder He is called the "God of all comfort" (2 Cor. 1:3) and the "Wonderful Counselor" (Isa. 9:6). He understands the agony of delinquency and divorce in a most realistic way and certainly not as one aloof and uninvolved. . . . The point to be noted is two-pronged. It first emphasizes that no distressed couple or bereft individual needs to approach God as though He were above such human problems and without sympathetic understanding. He is not just a censorious Judge, but a compassionate Friend. It also reminds us that such an attitude of understanding and redemptive mercy should likewise characterize the church, unless we have forgotten our redemptive mission. For us to fail to reflect God's attitude of mercy and restoration here is to invite His just judgment upon us, as Jesus declared (Matt. 7:2). God is in the business of helping people where they hurt, and we need to be about our Father's business.[15]

CHAPTER 5

Divorce and Your Child

If you have children, one of your major concerns will be the divorce's effect on them. Here are some guidelines that will help reduce your children's trauma.

Dr. Louise Despert, well-known child psychiatrist, has written an excellent book that every parent facing divorce should read. In *Children of Divorce*, Dr. Despert writes that parents should first take into consideration the age and sex of the children involved before telling them about the divorce. Only then, she writes, should the parents apply the following general guidelines:

1. Acknowledge that there has been a decision to separate. He already knows there is trouble, and to talk with you calmly and simply about the impending separation will help relieve his anxiety.

2. Acknowledge that grownups can make mistakes, and that his parents have made them. He must one day accept the fact that his parents are human; it is part of his growing up. You may be hurrying him a little, but the truth is a more durable basis for his confidence in you than deification of your god-like perfection which in any case cannot be maintained.

3. Assure him that he is in no way to blame for what has

happened between his parents. No matter what may have been said in anger or impatience, the trouble lies only between his parents and quite apart from him. In this way you help to relieve the guilt which most children take upon themselves when there is trouble between their parents.

But be careful in freeing him from blame, that you *do not by implication lay the blame upon someone else,* that is, upon each other. "Bad" and "good" are words which have no place in this discussion. *His parents simply do not get along with each other.* This period of your own emotional confusion is no time to make judgments, and certainly not to a child.

4. Finally and most important, assure him in every possible way that despite your differences with each other, you both still love him as you always have.[1]

Several times in her book, Dr. Despert cautions parents to make sure that they are going through with the separation or divorce before telling their child. But once you decide to separate or divorce, it's important to communicate with your child. Your child will already know that something is wrong between his mother and father, and silence about the problem is bound to raise his level of anxiety. In talking with your child, it's important that you strike a balance between being honest about what is happening and not burdening your child with details.

If you and your spouse have already separated, you might tell your child that "Mommy and Daddy are having some problems they are trying to work out. They will be living apart for a while so they can get over some of their bad feelings." In the case of a trial separation, set a date for the resumption of the marriage. Your child will pick up any indefiniteness that you have about it, regardless of your final decision.

DIVORCE AND THE INFANT

Mel Krantzler offers some helpful suggestions with regard to infants. He points out that when the child of divorce is an infant, he will pick up his mother's grief and depression.[2] The mother's mood is conveyed by changes in her pattern of care for the child. She may not be as relaxed or warm with the child, or the child may experience a change in her eating or sleeping patterns. He may react to all of this by changing his own eating, sleeping, or eliminating habits.

It's important, Krantzler writes, that the mother maintain the child's usual routine as closely as possible during this time. If she must change it because of the new demands on her—such as having to work—she should attempt to work out a new schedule that she can follow consistently. She must be careful not to convey a negative mood toward life and must avoid becoming too indulgent of the child. Although a mother, she also has a life of her own, and the baby must learn this.

DIVORCE AND THE PRESCHOOL CHILD

When the child of divorce is preschool age, he experiences both the loss of a parent and a break in his daily routine. He may temporarily revert to infantile behavior and lose bowel and bladder control, eat poorly, or have temper tantrums and nightmares. Anger and harsh discipline are not suitable in this situation. Your child is mourning too. You must be patiently firm and willing to spend more time helping the child relearn some lessons. But remember that this is his only way of reacting. You reacted too. Be on guard against the attitude that asks, *Why must I go through retraining my child at a time when I need all the cooperation from him that I can get?*

When the child is of later preschool age, he has begun to develop strong feelings toward the opposite-sex parent. Sometimes the child sees the same-sex parent as an obstacle to his relations with the opposite-sex parent and will secretly wish him dead. When the same-sex parent leaves, the child is often filled with guilt, believing that he has been responsible for the breakup. For this reason, many psychologists believe that frequent visits with the absent parent are helpful in getting the child to accept the fact that, although one parent has moved out, he [the child] is not at fault. He can also see that even though the other parent has moved out, his relationship with that parent hasn't ended.

Admittedly, frequent visits by the child to the noncustodial parent may put an added burden on both parents. They both may want to stay away from each other, and the child's visits keep them in contact. But gradually the child will get over his loss, and the parents will be able to disengage from frequent contact. This is one reason why it is important for the separation agreement to state clearly the terms under which the noncustodial parent will enjoy visiting rights.

DIVORCE AND THE PRIMARY CHILD

Following divorce, the primary-age child most frequently will live with the mother, who serves as the custodial parent. But whether the child lives with the father or mother, it must be remembered that the child views both parents as a single entity. The child has a difficult time thinking of parents as having lives and interests of their own apart from the functions of parenting. Mother is ever a mother and not a woman with her own individual needs. Father is ever a father and not a man with his own individual needs. So he needs to be assured that no matter what happens, the parent who is leaving still loves him and will continue to visit him. Remember, to the child, the mother and father are his *parents*. They are one. They may divorce each other, but they don't divorce him.

The child at this age is very insecure. He cannot make his way in the world and depends on parents who love him to do what is necessary to protect his welfare. Although a parent should avoid the perils of overindulgence or overprotectiveness, he should always remember that his young child depends on him for a sense of security.

When either the mother or father leaves the household, a child this age may persist in believing that he has somehow caused the departure and is no longer loved. Why else would either of them leave? It is important, then, that the child be assured that the problem is between mommy and daddy and that they are making each other unhappy. The child must be shown that his parents felt that they could be better parents by living apart and not making the home an unhappy place for him. He must understand that even though his parents are living apart, they will still be his mommy and daddy.

Dr. Despert suggests that the child be told that daddy (or

mommy, as the case may be) is feeling very unhappy. But the child should be told that mommy or daddy still loves him. If the child persists in wanting to know if daddy or mommy is coming back to see him, he should be assured that daddy or mommy will come to see him, but will live in his or her own house.

The child should have some idea of the arrangement by which the noncustodial parent will visit him. But parents should be very careful not to make promises they can't fulfill. It is far better for a child to receive a few promises that are kept than many promises that are not.

MIDDLE AND ADOLESCENT YEARS

Dr. Despert says that the child in his middle or adolescent years will have many of the same fears that the young child has, except that his fears will be a little more tangible—like the financial pinch of divorce or where he will spend his vacations. He also may be less inclined to talk about his problems. Often the child in this age group will brood and remain silent. He may daydream and show a marked decline in his school performance. Lecturing the child and "pumping" him for his feelings, as we've already seen, won't do any good during this stage of adjustment. Such actions will only make him angry and resentful. He will feel that you are intruding into his inner world. If he wanted you there, he would let you know.

I don't mean to imply that nothing should be done in this situation. You can voice what you think he is feeling. "You've been very quiet and withdrawn since dad and I broke up. I guess if I were a teen-ager who had just had his father move out, I'd feel the same way too. I just want you to know that I care."

If you say something like this, be prepared for an emotional outburst—anything from tears to anger. You may be blamed for the whole mess, but it won't do a bit of good to defend yourself. If you do, you can be sure that you'll drive your child deeper into himself.

Strangely, in intimate communication, facts are relatively unimportant to the child. The important thing is his feelings. No matter what the facts are, your child feels the way he feels, and from his point of view, justifiably so. The important question you must ask yourself at this point is, Do I still show acceptance, even though my child feels angry and hostile? You don't have to agree with your child's perspective in order to make him feel accepted. Yet, I'm not suggesting that you take issue with him. The important point is, *Can he feel the way he feels and still be accepted by you?* Most husbands and wives who divorce never learn to apply this principle to each other. Don't make the same mistake with your child.

Once your child knows that you still accept him in spite of his feelings, you have the basis of building a relationship on mutual respect. The day will come when he'll see "your side" more clearly. Remember, the important thing at this point is *not to defend your position;* you must make your child feel that he has been heard and understood, *no matter how incorrect you may feel his facts are.* Of course, if he wants to know what your position is, you may tell him. But be sure that you don't load him down with more details than would be wise to reveal or come across as defending yourself and trying to make your former spouse look bad. There is a big difference between reporting the events as you see them and defending yourself.

Krantzler offers similar views on how to communicate with a child in this age group.[3] He agrees that the school-age or preteen child of divorce needs to have his questions about the divorce answered. But the child should not be burdened with more than he has requested. Openness with the child, Krantzler stresses, is important. On one hand, the child needs to know about your feelings. On the other hand, he needs to be assured that things will remain pretty much the same for him—at least, as much as possible. Remember that a child is not sure what divorce is all about. All he knows is that it's *bad,* and he's heard enough about it to be afraid of what it's going to do to his life.

CHAPTER 6

Learning to Be a Single Parent

Being a parent is never easy. But it's even more difficult for a single parent. Suddenly you are burdened with a multitude of responsibilities. You may have to work full time, besides raising your children, keeping the house maintained, and cooking meals.

When asked what they do with their free time, some single parents will laugh scornfully and say, "What free time? I spend my whole life keeping job and home together. And when I'm done, I'm too pooped for anything else." If this describes your situation, you may still be angry and bitter. If you haven't gotten your negative feelings out therapeutically, by all means seek counseling. You must reach the place where the energy produced by your anger is directed toward fulfilling the mammoth task of single parenting.

TIME WITH YOUR CHILD

As you face your situation realistically, you will discover that the time and energy you have available for the children are limited. But since you can't give your children all the time you'd like, give them "quality" time. Find a few minutes each day, preferably when you're at your best, to give yourself to them. And when you must move on to other things, let them know why you must leave. They have other interests and will cultivate them if you make them feel secure in their new one-parent home.

In most two-parent homes, the parents expect the child to spend the majority of his time entertaining himself. Beware of falling into the subtle trap many solo parents fall into where you begin to think that you "owe" your child extra time because he has been "victimized" by divorce. If you dare give your child the slightest hint that this is the way you feel, he'll use it against you. A child is a manipulative creature. Like any human being, he looks for opportunities to turn a situation to his advantage. If *you* don't think of the child as the victim, *he* won't think of himself that way. If you convey to the child that *you* have a right to some fun in life, then *he* will accept the idea.

Remember, too, that in any normal home situation, meaningful contact between parent and child goes far beyond the moments you spend exclusively with the child. He learns much more information about the security of his situation by observing your work about the house and what you say on the telephone.

ATTITUDES TOWARD YOUR CHILDREN

As you begin to cope with your new life, don't think for a moment that you must walk around with a smile, singing all the time so your child will feel secure. The most realistic attitude you can have is, *Yes, it's tough being a solo parent, but we're going to make it just fine.* Such an attitude breeds reality and security for both you and the child at the same time.

I do not encourage insensitivity to the special burdens borne by the children of divorce. But don't make their problems worse by giving them the message that they are to be pitied because their parents are divorced. Some children wouldn't know they are to be pitied unless an unthinking parent told them! In view of this, it would be well to look at the types of parental behavior that jeopardize the adjustment of children.

The Guilty Parent

A divorced parent with children usually feels guilty because of what has happened to the children. The parent gives his children the message, "I have done a terrible thing to you by divorcing your father (or mother). You may make any demand on me, no matter how unreasonable, and I'm obliged to meet your demand as penance."

Any time you, the parent, give your child the verbal or nonverbal message that you have no right to set boundaries or no power to make decisions that affect the child, the child will exploit the situation. "I hate you for the terrible thing you did to me," the child will say. "If you really loved me, you would . . ." Indeed, you are actually inviting your child to exploit the situation. The child then becomes a problem, not because of the divorce, but because you have given him a message that reads, "You may behave abominably because I have unfairly subjected you to the loss of your father (or mother, as the case may be)."

As a parent, you should listen carefully to the child's statements and make him feel heard. But you should then give the child this very clear message. "I don't accept the verdict of guilty you have placed on me. I know that you miss your father (or mother), but life goes on for both of us. I want you to know right now that life is going to be as normal as I can make it under the circumstances, and I won't take any more nonsense from you now than I would if you had two parents living with you."

Parents who labor under the burden of guilt immobilize themselves from being the very parent the child needs during this time of emotional stress. When your child loses one resident parent through divorce, don't do him the disfavor of robbing him of both parents by becoming nonfunctional through guilt. It is obvious that children will exploit the guilt feelings of parents. This occurs in both two-parent and one-parent households. Don't play the game. If you have difficulty identifying manipulations, read Everett Shostrom's book, *Man the Manipulator*.[1]

This does not mean that you should become callous about your feelings or hide them. You will feel angry and hurt at times. But there's nothing wrong with letting your child know how *you* feel too, just so long as you don't also play a manipulative game—the game of "martyr." The reality of the situation is that your child hurts and you hurt. But life must go on, and it goes on best where there is mutual understanding and respect. You are not asking your child to become a substitute parent or to accept responsibilities he normally wouldn't accept. Rather, you are rightfully asking your child to respect your needs as a human being—a very important message to *all* children which is essential to their socialization.

You do well to remember that not all your child's problems are the result of divorce. Every normal two-parent household has its share of problem children, including everything from bed-wetting to poor grades in school. Avoid whipping yourself with reproach, thinking that your child is having problems because of you. The child may have had the problem anyway.

The Permissive Parent

One common manifestation of guilt is permissiveness. Not only does the parent feel that he has no right to disagree with the child or say no to his wishes, he often hopes that he can buy the child's favor with special treats. Parents will often permit the child to do things or will grant favors that they would never dream of granting in a normal two-parent home.

Fathers are especially guilty of this. They hold out a bigger lollipop than mom does and say, "See how much better things can be when you're with me," or "See what a better person I am than mom, who is always saying 'no' or 'you can't.'" Dad, if you are the noncustodial parent, your children need to see, more than anything else, your example of a normal, well-adjusted male. This is true for both sons and daughters. Both male and female children will derive their ideas of maleness by what you do or do not do. Your daughter depends on having her femininity validated by you, the most important male in her life. She needs *you*, not your gifts or promises of a better life with you. She needs to know that you think she is going to grow up to be one fantastic female. Your son, on the other hand, needs to know how men relate to people in particular and life in general. For instance, what does it mean to be a male? Does it mean that a man is an ever-promising but nondelivering, insensitive blowhard? Or does it mean that he is more concerned with people and their feelings than with things?

The achieving father often finds it easier to deliver things (or at least the promise of things) than to deliver himself as a warm, sensitive person. This does not mean that mothers are guilt-less. When Mom has a good job, she may fall into the same temptation, finding it less emotionally draining to give the children things instead of spending quality time with them.

When teen-agers are going through a divorce, they will often forcefully press for a relaxation of rules. This is not unusual even in the two-parent home, but it may become a crucial issue in the broken home. Divorced parents often knuckle under the pressure and relax rules indiscriminately, thinking that this is what the child wants. Often, testing boundaries and bucking rules is the child's way of seeing how secure and stable his situation is. The wise parent sets reasonable rules and boundaries, and when he enforces them, the child develops a sense of security. He discovers that some very certain things exist in his home where things were once very uncertain.

The enforcement of rules must not, however, be undertaken with hysterical desperation (which is a sign of weakness and uncertainty on the part of the parent). Enforcing the established rules with quiet confidence conveys the attitude of stability. The message to the child must be, "Yes, your father (or mother) and I have divorced. But this doesn't mean that now life is suddenly in chaos and that there are no longer any rules or guidelines. Life will continue to go on in the pattern that it has—as much as we are able to make it that way. Divorce does not mean disaster for the family or desperation for me—your parent. Now this is what I expect of you . . ."

Every household, divorced or not, must follow the common sense principle of balance between the opinions, needs, and wants of your children and your own opinions, needs, and wants. And if you can't agree on where the balance is, then you had better talk about it with your children—respecting both your position and theirs.

The Overprotective Parent

Sometimes lack of common sense is seen in the overprotective parent. In a normal two-parent setting, this type of parent might behave quite differently and realize that children must face certain rigors of life by themselves or with little direction from parents. Following a divorce, however, the custodial parent may suddenly become overly protective of the child, to the point that the child is not permitted to go through the normal rigors of growing up. If you are like this, ask yourself, *What would I do if my former husband (or wife) were still on the scene?* If you don't know what you'd do, simply because you depended on your former spouse's advice on the matter, discuss it with a trusted friend who is of the same sex as your former spouse. Or, if the relationship with your former spouse is amiable, discuss the matter with him (or her). Yes, your child has experienced the pain of divorce. Don't make matters worse by raising him as a pitiful creature who must be protected from the rigors of life because he has "already suffered enough pain."

The Excuse-making Parent

It's a well-established fact that the manner in which you and your spouse break the news of divorce to your child is very important. You should make it clear that the child is not to blame for the divorce (though he may insist he is) and that the child "will continue to see mommy and daddy" even though they won't be living together. But after you have both told the child about the divorce and separation that has taken place, don't go further and communicate unreal pictures of the situation to your child.

In the interest of not belittling the noncustodial parent (a proper motive), the custodial parent may foster an unreal image of the absent parent: take, for example, the case of the absent father who always makes big promises but never comes through. Mother knows that he's just a big blowhard who spends most of his life trying to impress people but never delivering. Naturally, he treats his children the same way. On one hand, she does well not to cut him down, but on the other, she does her children a disservice by making excuses for him. The reality of the matter should be clearly stated: "Daddy has problems just like you and I do. He has a problem with making promises that he doesn't keep. We really shouldn't get angry with daddy because he's like this. We feel sorry for him that he hurts us with broken promises, but we can avoid being hurt if we understand that he has this problem." In such a situation, daddy does not become the biggest bum in the world, nor is he the most wonderful person in the world. He is a real person who, like everyone, has virtues and faults.

A child becomes confused, and rightly so, when his absent parent is represented to him inadequately. *If he is the good, well-meaning person that you always represent him to be,* the child may think, *then why did you divorce him?* As the child matures and observes what you and the absent parent are really like, he will have a better understanding of why you divorced.

The Happy Holidays Parent

The happy holidays parent is well-meaning, but unaware of the effects of his good intentions. Whenever a holiday, birthday, or special occasion arises, this parent feels it necessary to invite the noncustodial parent to the celebration. The thoughtfulness is to be praised because, after all, such times are really family times that should be enjoyed by all. But the reality of the matter is that the re-creation of the family's happy holidays may create a false hope of reconciliation in the child.

Unless the marriage was extremely hard on them, most children harbor a desire to reestablish the family. When mom and dad come together again on a special occasion and are on their best behavior, they may give the child false hope. It is far better that the child celebrate these special events separately with each parent. Then, of course, each parent must be careful not to try to outdo the other with a lavish celebration. Such competition is just another form of the "lollipop war."

Often children grown to adulthood are perplexed about their wedding plans, especially if either parent has remarried. The children should not be afraid to say how *they* would like their parents to participate in the wedding. This is their day. The parents do well to respect their wishes. If they don't want to participate as the children wish, then they should make it clear in as open and sensitive a way as possible.

DEVELOPING YOUR CHILD'S IDENTITY

I'm not trying to ignore the fact that children need a mother/father, husband/wife, and male/female image to become adequately socialized. In a normal two-parent home, children gather their ideas about these dimensions of human relations from the models they see in their parents. In divorce, when such models are unavailable, the child wonders, *How do mother/father, husband/wife, and male/female relationships function?* If the child's sex is different from that of the custodial parent, he may wonder, *How does a person of my sex relate to people in general? What does it mean to be an adult person of my sex?*

The custodial parent must remember that he cannot fill the role of both parents. If he tries, he may not fill the role of either parent. A mother can't fill the role of a father, and a father can't fill the role of a mother. But substitutes outside the home can be found.

Ideally, the child should receive the model of his sexual identity from the same-sex parent, since a lot of weight is given to family identity. But in the absence of adequate family models for your children, you should provide your child with models outside the home. Sometimes sports activities for boys and girls in which coaches and their families participate can provide helpful models. You might attend church activities where your child can observe well-adjusted relationships. Your children could also be included in the activities of other families. At any rate, whether or not the child's own noncustodial parent provides an adequate same-sex model, don't be reluctant to augment it with other models.

This doesn't mean that you should always be involving your child with a same-sex adult. Again, common sense should rule the day. What would you do if you had a normal two-parent home? Sometimes your child will want to play with his friends and will not want activity with an adult. Respect this need as much as the child's need for privacy. As your child moves through adolescence, he will look for more privacy and will attempt to keep his problems to himself and solve them in his own way. His peer group will have a great influence on him at this time. And in the loneliness following divorce, the child may seek even greater closeness with peers whom he feels understand. As with any household, you'd better be sure that you know who your child's friends are and what kind of households are modeling behavior for him. You have a responsibility to veto any friendships that you feel are not a healthy influence on him. You would have this responsibility whether or not you were divorced.

Special Parental Concerns

When their child has been subjected to the stress of divorce, parents voice particular concerns. Among those most frequently mentioned are delinquency, homosexuality, the young child who will not sleep alone, and a decline in school performance.

Delinquency

We are repeatedly told that divorce is a major cause of juvenile delinquency. Yet, citing a study of approximately 18,000 delinquent children, Dr. Despert points out that only one-tenth of the delinquent boys and about one-fifth of the delinquent girls came from families broken by separation or divorce. Where, then, are the delinquents coming from? Dr. Despert writes:

> Not, we may be sure, from well-adjusted families in which both parents were on the job. Some came from homes broken by the death of a parent, but not a large proportion, as we know from other studies. Some are the product of homes broken by desertion; these figures do not appear in the statistics as legal separations. But the largest proportion of these children who fall foul

of the law come from families which are emotionally broken, *without* having their disharmony overtly recognized by a recourse to law.[2]

Emotional divorce—disharmony that goes on and on—is the culprit, not the actual parting. A child placed in this situation actually finds a measure of relief when the break comes. At least the daily confrontations end. Even though a child should have the benefit of two parents, he can be raised successfully by one parent. As I suggested earlier, the custodial parent should see to it that the child is exposed to a parental model of the opposite sex.

Homosexuality

Many divorcing or divorced parents fear that their bad marriage might have a toxic effect on their child, particularly in the area of sexual development. Fortunately, divorce in and of itself does not produce a climate for the development of a homosexual. Rather, what goes on at home and what is left out of the relationship tend to be the precipitating factors.

The parent who has special interest in this problem will want to read Peter and Barbara Wyden's book, *Growing Up Straight*. The Wydens cite three primary factors that contribute to the development of a homosexual child: (1) creation of impaired gender identity; (2) fear of the opposite sex; and (3) opportunity for sexual release with a member of the same sex. (This third factor alone, however, will not create a committed homosexual.)[3]

Anything you do to make your child feel that his or her own sex is undesirable may make the child avoid identifying with that gender. You must carefully follow these three basic guidelines: (1) don't weaken your child's sense of masculinity or femininity; (2) don't create in your child a fear of the opposite sex or fail to accept his or her sexuality; (3) be aware of your own sexual hangups and be willing to deal with them. Sexually healthy parents produce sexually healthy children.

The Mother's Responsibility

The mother who gains custody of a son must be careful how

she handles herself. It is normal for children to show sexual interest in the opposite-sex parent, but the parent must handle such interest carefully. If the mother is fearful of her son's expressions of his sexuality, for example, she may deal with them by reducing his masculinity and encouraging effeminate attitudes. Fearful of a male/female relationship in a home without a husband, she may give her son the distinct message that she wishes he were not a boy. Or, feeling deeply the loneliness of divorce, she may make her son a substitute companion who must leave his male sexuality out of the relationship.

Usually a homosexual boy's mother is overprotective, excessively intimate ("come close, but leave your sexuality out"), and domineering of the father, usually in a deprecating manner. The manner in which the divorce is secured and how she treats and speaks of the father after the divorce ("that no-good bum") may serve to strengthen the bad effect even more. Not only does this type of mother impair the gender identity of the son by refusing to recognize him as a male, but she also gives the message that men are no good ("look at your father, for example!"). The implication of the mother's message to the boy who is looking for his sexual identity is "Don't become a man."

As I mentioned earlier, it is important that the mother be balanced in what she says about the father to the boy. The father may truly be a no-good bum. But it doesn't help the boy to hear mom say this. She might simply tell her son that his father has problems and that he will find out what those problems are soon enough on his own.

The Father's Responsibility

The influence of a destructive mother can be countered by a father who is strong and does not permit the child's development to be smothered. The Wydens go so far as to say that a father has absolute veto power over the homosexual development of his son. Even though a father may not be the custodial parent, he still can have an important influence on his son's development by maintaining contact with him.[4]

The most helpful father is sure of his male identity and is

constructive, supportive, and warm toward his son. On the other hand, a father who is unsure of his male identity or panic-stricken about his son's seeming lack of male identity may become demanding, cruel, and demeaning. Fathers have been known to say the cruelest thing of all—to imply that their son is becoming a woman by living with his mother.

The most natural reaction a son will have to this second kind of father is, *If that's manhood, I don't want it.* And if his mother reinforces his father's message by saying, "Don't be a man," the son is in serious trouble.

The son needs a male model who is pleasant to be around and respected by his mother as much as is possible under the circumstances. But the father must also be around. His visitation privileges must be taken seriously, not only to assure the child that his father still loves him, but also to give the child a male model to copy. Remember, our children learn far more by watching us and listening to what we say than they do through formal instruction. If the father can't be around, the mother must give the child a clear message that it's okay for him to become a man and point out some good male models whom they both know and respect.

The father who senses that the mother prefers the son over him may complicate the problem by becoming hostile toward the son. He may demonstrate his hostility by rejecting his son verbally or by showing indifference toward him. The son will receive the message that he is taking his father's place in his mother's affections and may feel that he must show his father that he is not a male threat by not being a male.

When a father has the custody of a daughter, he faces the same conflict with the daughter that the mother faces with the son—incest taboo. The father is in a position to authenticate his daughter's femininity by being affectionate and masculine. The father who is afraid of his feelings may discount his daughter's femininity as a way of dealing with his own fears. Consequently he may give his daughter the message that her womanhood is repulsive or dangerous, and she will probably avoid womanhood at all cost.

The father may also be tempted to malign the opposite sex.

Speaking out of his own hurt, he may give his daughter the message that women are no good. The girl may take him seriously and oblige him by not allowing her womanhood to develop fully.

Fear of Sleeping Alone

Another problem you may face both during and after your divorce is a young child's fearfulness of sleeping in his own room. Dr. Despert suggests that the child's bed may be moved into the parent's room temporarily.[5] The child should not, however, be allowed to sleep in bed with you. There is nothing wrong, of course, with the child's crawling into bed with you for a bedtime story. But separate beds will minimize the development of too great an intimacy.

An alternative to moving the child's bed into your bedroom is to let the child sleep on a pallet on the floor. By doing this, you will give your child the clear message that the arrangement is only temporary. The child's place is in his own bed, in his own bedroom. Also, by having the child sleep on the floor, you make the arrangement physically uncomfortable for the child. The child will soon learn that he prefers the comfort of his own bed. When he complains that he is not comfortable, warmly suggest that he move back into his own room.

Another option, Dr. Despert suggests, is to move into the child's bedroom.[6] The child will eventually tell you to move out, probably through a very indirect message. "You keep me awake at night when you move around" would be one example. Anything suggesting that the child is not comfortable with you in his room may be your opportunity to suggest that perhaps you should move back into your own room. If he suggests that you move his bed into your room, simply tell him that his bed belongs in his own room. This gentle message lets him know that you're willing to go along with his presence in your room, but that you're not willing to have him move in.

Slipping Grades

Some children react to a divorce by doing poorly in school or by becoming a behavior problem. This often occurs long before the actual divorce. Sometimes it is the child's attempt to focus attention on himself so that his parents will work together in his behalf. This may be the child's way of asking, "Do you really care about me?" It is extremely unwise to hassle a child about his poor performance at this time. You know all too well that the emotional impact of the divorce is making it difficult for you to concentrate. It is no easier on the child and may even be more difficult for him.

When parents become preoccupied with their own lives, whether in marriage or in divorce, their child needs assurance. In a divorce, the child needs to know that, although the marriage is over, his parents still care about him. Often just giving sincere attention to the child is enough to get him to change his behavior and his grades.

This principle of parental concern holds especially true in counseling. Children of divorced parents are frequently brought for counseling because of poor grades. While there is often a need for better management of the child at home or school, or a need for tutoring, children improve simply because the parent or parents were concerned enough about the situation to seek counseling with the child.

During the divorce, your child's emotional and social adjustment are the most important things to consider. His grades may slip, but he can pick up the work another time. Your child will need to spend a lot of time figuring out what happened. He will ask himself if he's to blame and decide how secure his future is.

As you pick up clues from time to time about what's going on in your child's mind by the questions he asks, remember that all the questions are important and must not be brushed aside. The questions may seem foolish from your frame of reference, but to your child they make a great deal of sense. I'm not encouraging you to go into great detail about what happened or what the future holds: you may not know what the future holds. But you should be reassuring nevertheless. You may have to tell your child that you can't answer all of his questions, but if you take a positive attitude toward the future, your child will also cultivate a positive attitude.

When your child begins to feel secure in his home and surroundings, his schoolwork will pick up again. This does not minimize the need for the child to get his homework done. He may need tutoring, or he may need to stay after school to understand the work he didn't grasp in class. Many children from well-adjusted homes also need that kind of help. But remember not to make an issue of his grades, for they may be just a symptom of his preoccupation with the divorce.

CHAPTER 7

Dealing With the
Emotional Pain of Divorce

Feelings of abandonment, rejection, grief, self-pity, anger, failure, guilt, and conflict with religious convictions frequently rush in on the separated or divorced person. Such feelings aren't easily sorted out, either. One provokes another. Rejection provokes anger and self-pity. Abandonment raises fear. Grief, guilt, and self-pity go round and round in an exhausting whirlpool of emotion, stirring up old feelings of anger.

Though it's difficult to sort out these emotions, let's try. Let's look at each one and try to understand it. Where do these emotions come from? How do they interrelate? What can be done about them?

REJECTION AND ABANDONMENT

Although these two emotions are quite different, they are so closely related that they must be studied together. Rejection has to do with personal devaluation. By divorcing you someone is saying hurtful things to you. The hurt may not come out in so many words. In fact, your spouse might be very civil about the whole thing. But by divorcing you, your spouse seems to be saying, "You're worthless," "Whatever you once had, you've lost it," "I have better things to do with my life than spend it with you," or "You're a miserable failure as a human being." Even if you initiate divorce, you still feel your spouse's rejection.

Like every human being, you need a feeling of self-worth. But no trauma quite damages that feeling like the rejection caused by divorce. Divorce may leave you believing that there is absolutely nothing redeemable about you. Following your feelings of rejection, you will probably have feelings of abandonment and become terrified of being alone. This is true for men as well as women. And when rejection and abandonment are put together, they mean double jeopardy. *It's bad enough to be alone,* you think, *but when I'm also made to feel absolutely worthless, how do I cope with being alone?*

The answer is not a simple one. These emotions do not heal with the usual emotional Band-Aids dispensed by friends. The usual response—the reassurances that you really are a worthwhile person followed by a summary of your achievements—doesn't do any good. No matter what people say, your logical response is, "If I'm such a great person, why did he (or she) reject me?"

The fact is that you are not dealing with logic here; you are dealing with emotions. Any time you have been emotionally committed to a relationship where you are giving of yourself and are receiving emotional strength, you will experience this feeling when you are rejected.

This principle is true in friendships as well as in marriage. Couples who live together rather than getting married, for example, don't avoid the trauma of divorce when they break up. Whether or not a couple is married, when they live together they form an emotional commitment to their relationship that makes a breakup traumatic. And sometimes, because a commitment was never formalized by marriage, the trauma is worse. Often the response, especially for women, is, *What a fool I've been. I've given of myself, and he walks away leaving me with absolutely nothing. I've been used.*

The issue of self-worth (which is the real issue in rejection and abandonment) is especially difficult for a woman who is divorced. This is mainly due to the fact that her identity and financial security were probably based on those of her husband. She wasn't known as Roberta Eggnatz, computer programmer; she was known as Mrs. Horace Eggnatz, housewife. Not only did her identity come from being married to this man, but she also derived no financial security in being Mr. Horace Eggnatz's cook, housekeeper, laundress, seamstress, errand-runner, mother of his children, and lover. She was also dependent, to a large or small degree, on her husband's income. I'm not saying that men are free from the pain of rejection and abandonment that women feel after divorce. But in many cases, men are able to maintain a larger measure of self-worth and dignity through their work than their former spouses, who had to quit working full time to raise a family.

In order to shake this terrible feeling of rejection and abandonment as a divorced person, you must recognize your self-worth as a single person. Yes, you do have to buck a couple-oriented society, but remember that *single people are worth-while too.* If you're a woman whose identity and financial security were in her former husband, it's going to be tough to regain your identity and security as a single person, especially if it has been years since you were single and worked. Recovery from your feelings of rejection and abandonment may take anywhere from six months to two years. But time is your ally.

Every day that you live as a single person, you will become more comfortable with the idea of being single. Each success that you have as a single person will be an investment in your feelings of self-worth. There is no such thing as instant relief from feelings of rejection and abandonment, and to look for it is unrealistic. You must actively throw yourself into the job of being single, and you must permit time to bring healing. But above all, you must be *willing* to be a healed person, rather than an ever-grieving divorced person. Just as some people never recover from physical handicaps because they refuse to accept them, so some people never recover after a divorce because they refuse to accept singleness. Beware of this temptation.

You may ask, however, "Why do people choose to hang onto

their hurt?" They do so for a very good reason. Most frequently, they receive a "payoff"—a positive benefit. And what positive benefit might be gained? Safety from being hurt again. For example, if you have been hurt in a love relationship, you can hang onto that hurt and use it as an excuse to avoid further love relationships. You can use the hurt to become silent and withdrawn or to become angry and bitter. Either way, by hanging onto the hurt, you create distance from other people.

Not everyone who feels abandonment and rejection after a divorce uses those feelings to avoid relationships. Certainly there is a normal period of grief and mourning. But when the hurt goes on year after year, something's wrong.

The Mourning Game

I remember one divorcee, Sandy, who had been extremely dependent on her former husband. He had taken care of the income tax return, servicing the car, maintaining the house, banking, investments, paying bills, and anything that involved contact with the business world outside the home. When Sandy's husband divorced her, she fell into a depression that lasted for years.

Finally one counselor figured out the game she was playing and alerted her family and friends. By emphasizing her "pitiful" state and remaining depressed, Sandy had developed an excellent way to avoid fulfilling the responsibilities and tasks her former husband had undertaken. When her counselor and friends stopped playing the game with her—doing for her what she should have been doing for herself—she became furious. After a few months of playing suicide games, however, she finally decided to take on the responsibilities that she had been avoiding.

Suicide Games

These are the deadly games that people play to whip others into line: "I'll kill myself if you don't do what I want." People who play these games don't intend to kill themselves, but they may die because their plan to be saved from death doesn't work out. They expect someone to find them in a comatose state, perhaps, and that someone doesn't show up. Or a supposedly "safe" suicide attempt turns out to be very lethal. When people play at suicide, they may miscalculate and end the game.

GRIEF

Grief is the spontaneous response to the loss of a relationship, and can be the result of abandonment and rejection. Losing a spouse through divorce produces a reaction of grief similar to that which death produces. In divorce, a relationship has died. There's a sense of loss, no matter how bad the relationship might have been. A grieving individual tends to forget all the bad in the relationship and remember only the good. Grieving divorced persons often say, "I know the relationship was not good, but why do I miss him so?" Bad marriages, like bad habits, are hard to shake. Though destructive, they are at least familiar company and their loss creates a vacuum. And people, as with all of nature, try to fill that vacuum—even to the extent of trying to revive a dead marriage.

Grief, then, is your emotional response to the vacuum created by either death or divorce. Be on guard. Before you learn to accept your grief, you will probably deny your loss. You will think, *This really isn't happening to me.* Denial, a normal human defense against a trauma too painful to accept, gradually gives way to the acceptance of reality in the normal course of life. You have your own pace at which you face reality. When you are ready to face and accept your status as a single person, you will be ready for grief and mourning—the painful acceptance of reality. Bit by bit, you will look at the totality of your loss and will accept it with courage and growing optimism about the future.

Watch out for denial that doesn't end. This kind of denial actually inhibits grief and mourning. It refuses to let you face the reality of your loss. Mel Krantzler writes:

> Such denial is dangerous. Mourning will take place in any event; if denied or suppressed, however, its healing powers will not be effectively utilized. To restore physiological and emotional balance we must accept all the feelings engendered by a loss. These are not always pleasant feelings. In even the most loving relationship, loss will produce in the survivor strong

hostility toward the one who has left. Rationally this may not make sense; emotionally we feel abandoned. We feel guilty over real or imagined instances of acts performed or not performed during the past, knowing they can never be set to rights now. These feelings are produced in the most harmonious relationship. In an ambivalent union characterized by large components of love *and* hate, attraction *and* fear, dependency *and* resentment, the negative emotions of the survivor experiences—together with the loss of the familiar role and habits of being husband or wife—may prove too terrifying to recognize or accept. He or she then retreats to fantasies in which the absent partner is still present and life is as it was before.

The mourning process provides a way for us to ventilate all these conflicting feelings—a ventilation for our growth into independent persons. Its effect is to heal our psychic wounds so that we can then free ourselves from entrapment in the past and start the process of living constructively in the present.[1]

The toughest time in dealing with denial is at the onset of holidays. I always experience a surge in my client load before and after holidays by both the about-to-be-divorced and the divorced. Holidays are traditional family times and reveal the health or sickness of the family. Before the holidays, family members scurry to patch things up so that the coming celebration may be more pleasant than those in times past. After the holidays, though, an air of desperation remains. The feeling expressed by defeated couples is "Once again we bombed. This holiday was no better than the last." Christmas and New Year's Day are particularly difficult when a marriage is dying or dead. When things have been bad, the thinking is, *Not only did I have a very unmerry Christmas, I also expect to have a very unhappy New Year.* The important thing to remember when you encounter these difficulties is that you *must* face the realities of your situation. Denial of them is dangerous; such indulgence will lead to self-pity.

SELF-PITY

People who indulge themselves in self-pity have led me to two discoveries in my counseling.

First, self-pity is an attempt to insulate oneself against reality and all the pain that reality holds. This insulation is made of the most basic material of fantasy. *This shouldn't have happened to me. What ought to be happening is . . .* I must now stress the difference between mourning and self-pity. A mourning individual *faces* the reality that his relationship has died. The individual immersed in self-pity, on the other hand, *refuses to face* that reality. A mourning individual *accepts* the death of his relationship, while the self-pitying individual *rejects* the reality that his relationship has died and lives in a fantasy world. He then uses self-pity as an excuse to avoid other relationships that might lead to future hurt.

Second, self-pity gives the hurting individual self-comforting strokes and may also be a way of getting comforting strokes from others. Mourning may bring some comforting strokes from others, but is more involved with the process of facing and accepting reality. After a time, mourning ceases and circumstances are fully accepted and made a thing of the past. Self-pity, on the other hand, is ongoing; there is no end to it. It's like an addiction to a painkiller that continues long after healing should have taken place.

Whether you are indulging in self-pity or know someone who is, realize that self-pity is a difficult game to break up. If, as a friend, you sympathize with such a person, you reinforce his self-pity. But if you draw the line on how much you will sympathize, you also run the risk of alienating yourself from the very person you're trying to help. If you are trapped in a game like this, it often helps simply to describe the dilemma in a nonjudgmental way. If you are guilty of self-pity, realize that it is a way of avoiding reality.

ANGER

Divorced people often surprise themselves with the anger they express over the death of the marriage relationship. Normally placid, religiously committed people even find themselves swearing violently at the divorcing spouse. Even when the person has initiated the divorce action, the anger is still there. Often the expressed or unexpressed feeling is "Why didn't you listen to me when I told you that our marriage was in trouble?"

Constructive Anger

I'm coming more and more to the conviction that constructive anger is one of the emotions that God has given us to help us face otherwise intolerable situations. Constructive anger produces a positive physiological reaction. It starts our adrenalin flowing, which in turn produces both the *desire* to do something about the problem and the *energy* to begin working toward a solution. When we feel we have been unjustly treated or have not received our due, this type of anger may prompt us to spring into action and do for ourselves what we have been waiting for someone else to do. Instead of moaning "Poor me" and doing nothing about the bad situation, a person with the capacity for constructive anger can say, "How can you do this to me?" He can then deal with the situation. When the action he takes as a result of the initial anger is constructive, then it can be said that his anger is constructive.

I want to make it clear that anger can be very destructive if permitted to express itself destructively. The Bible recognizes the difference between constructive and destructive kinds of anger. In Ephesians 4:26, for example, we are urged to be angry. "Be angry," the passage reads, "and yet do not sin; do not let the sun go down on your anger." The simple truth of this verse is that anger which is not dealt with can lead to a different type of anger that is sinful. This sinful anger comes as a result of our unexpressed emotions and sometimes leads to depression. Whatever our reasons for feeling angry, we must deal with our anger openly and quickly.

Unfortunately many Christians and other religiously committed people consider anger to be an unspiritual emotion and totally reject it. When I point out to people that Jesus became angry with the Pharisees on more than one occasion, they respond, "Jesus wasn't angry; He was righteously indignant." Call it what you will, but it still adds up to a very constructive use of anger. The Old Testament abounds with the principle that God's people are to hate what God hates and to be angry with those things that anger Him. And when I read the account of Jesus' second coming in Revelation 19:11-21, I don't envision a Sunday school picnic. I read about the Son of God wearing a garment drenched with blood, wielding a sword that slashes, ruling men with an iron rod that smashes. I read about anger and retribution.

"So how does constructive anger help me now?" you may be asking. First, realize that the experience of anger is a result of the experience of intimacy. The moment we permit ourselves to get close to someone and become emotionally dependent on him, we expose ourselves to disappointment and hurt. But we also expose ourselves to the possibility of growth. The growth comes when we receive the maximum benefits of someone else's support and give our own support in return. But since no one can give at all times without making mistakes, anger occurs. Someone ends up feeling that he has given too much and received too little in return.

In a constructive relationship, this anger can lead to constructive discussion on how the proper balance could be achieved—how both may receive maximum benefit from each other's support without neglecting self-support. In a destructive relationship, the anger will remain unexpressed, until it leads to distance and withdrawal when both people involved want to avoid repeated, unresolved hurt. Psychiatrist Jay Kuten, in *Coming Together—Coming Apart*,[2] sums up this point well when he says that anger can either sharpen a relationship or grind it down.

Dangers of Unexpressed Anger

At the risk of oversimplification, I'll define depression as unexpressed anger turned inward on the self. Depressed people find it difficult to express their anger at others, so they express it toward themselves. This is particularly true when the depression is the result of some loss.

Every person needs to feel to some degree that he is good, impressive, rich, and powerful. Or, to put it in a word, self-worthy. Depression often comes when we experience a loss of self-worth. We then become angry at ourselves for making or allowing the loss to happen and become lonely because of some terrible thing *we* have done or left undone or because we feel ugly in body or in behavior. But this type of depressed or passive anger, instead of making our adrenalin flow, actually has the opposite effect and makes us feel withdrawn and listless. In order to change our attitudes and get rid of our anger, we must turn this passive form of anger into a more active form, as I described earlier. When we convert passive anger into active anger by expressing it, we are in a better position to look more objectively at our "terrible mistakes."

FEELINGS OF FAILURE

The following statement, from a pamphlet prepared by the Conciliation Court of Sonoma County's Superior Court, in California, is an example of the burden of failure society places on the separated or divorced person.

> Failure is not a popular American word, yet every divorce statistic means two people have failed in life's most noble and important relationship—failed themselves, failed their children, failed their Creator, and failed society.
>
> Because our experience proves that most unhappy marriages are merely sick and can be made healthy and happy again, we don't want your marriage to be just another failure.[3]

The burden is even greater if you are a separated or divorced Christian who has heard all your life how wrong divorce is. Both society and the church would then seem to be aligned against you. How tragic, especially when you may well be the unwilling party to a divorce or have spent hours in counseling looking for some way to salvage your marriage.

How I wish, as a marriage counselor, that I could tell the Christian placed in this situation that if he would only do this or that, his marriage would work. I can't. It takes two people to make a marriage work, and both of them must be committed to their relationship and willing to do whatever is required to make it work. No person, whether he is a Christian or not, can do it alone. Yes, he may subject himself to the outrageous demands of his spouse and knuckle under, but that's not a marriage. That's subservience to tyranny in an attempt to keep the myth of the marriage alive. And even that doesn't always keep marriage partners together. Often, no matter what an individual does, he cannot save his marriage.

"Why do people brand me with failure?" one man asked bitterly. As I listened, I agreed with him. Such a judgment was an outrage, especially in view of the heroic efforts that he had made. I have far from a 100 percent success rate in marriage counseling, but when a marriage cannot be salvaged, I try to send the client away with the feeling that he has done everything he possibly could do to salvage the marriage. I don't mean to imply that the feelings of failure separated or divorced people encounter are never justified. I only object to this epithet being hurled indiscriminately at everyone who is separated or divorced. If failure is a justified description of one's unsuccessful attempt at marriage, then let's look at how you can handle this painful emotion constructively.

For the purpose of illustration, let's say that you justifiably feel that you have failed in your marriage. Are you going to give yourself up to a life of grief, or are you going to mourn the loss and learn from your mistakes? This isn't the first time you have failed at something big, nor will it be your last. Are you going to look at your failure constructively and ask yourself, *What can I learn from all this?* Your mental attitude toward this experience is extremely important. You must try to come to the place in your life where you can view your failures as learning experiences. Someone once said, "People who do not learn from their failures are bound to repeat them."

GUILT

Feelings of guilt are closely related to feelings of failure. And, like the feeling of failure, the feeling of guilt may or may not be justifiable. If, for example, you feel guilty because you truly and objectively did make a significant contribution to the demise of your marriage, your guilt would be justifiable. Unjustifiable guilt, on the other hand, would be the guilt you might feel simply because your marriage failed. Since being separated or divorced is socially and religiously unacceptable, you feel guilty for being that way.

In one sense, justifiable guilt might be considered the

easiest of the two types to handle. If you have blown it, you might become a better person through the lessons learned and you might use your guilt constructively to change your behavior. But in the case of unjustifiable, false guilt—feeling guilty for joining the ranks of the divorced against your will— you're faced with what may appear to be an irresolvable guilt.

The Perpetuation of False Guilt

False guilt is perpetuated in two ways. First, it's perpetuated by the words and actions of others who say, in essence, "You should not be divorced. You're guilty before God and society." Of course you're going to feel guilty when these accusations are laid on you! And this guilt is borne most often by people whose parents manipulated them with false guilt as they grew up. With such people, guilt is a way of life, and they quickly react to unfair judgments.

When you become divorced—or if you are divorced—you will learn that others will try to place false guilt on you by their actions and attitudes. When those whom you respect and love give you the message, "You are wrong for what you have done," your immediate reaction will be to feel guilty. This is why it's important for you to establish, to your own satisfaction before God, the biblical basis for divorce. Men have their opinions, but God ultimately is the judge.

If you can honestly say that you're not imposing the guilt on yourself, then see if it's being imposed on you—deliberately or otherwise—by other people. A former spouse who is attempting to justify himself in order to look good in the eyes of others will make you look bad and feel guilty. Perhaps your children make you feel guilty and upset because the divorce has displaced or inconvenienced them. Again, their intent may not be to make you feel guilty. But the thoughtless voicing of their own unhappiness can produce the same result.

In fairness to family and relatives, it should also be said that their reactions of embarrassment, awkwardness, or silence may not always stem from feelings of judgment. They may be at a loss to know what to do or say or how to react. One divorcé who discussed this later with a friend learned that he had been in this dilemma. "When you told me of your divorce," the friend said, "I didn't know whether to congratulate you or commiserate with you."

I had a similar experience. After my mother died, my father remarried. I was thirty-eight at the time and performed the ceremony. But I distinctly recall my awkwardness in talking to or writing to my stepmother. I didn't want to call her "mother," because I felt that this would be dishonoring to my real mother. I didn't want to call her by her first name, because that seemed disrespectful. In writing, I felt strange addressing the letter to Mr. and Mrs. R. A. Bustanoby. True, she was Mrs. R. A. Bustanoby, but so had been my mother. As I look back on this, it seems strange that a thirty-eight-year-old man of reasonable intelligence and education should have had difficulty in deciding how to address his new mother. But it's not so strange when you realize that this problem had little to do with intelligence or education. It was purely an emotional issue. I finally got used to the idea that she was indeed Mrs. R. A. Bustanoby, and to take that away would be a gross injustice to her and a denial that she was rightly married to my father. I am now comfortable calling her by her first name, since "mother" doesn't really fit and "stepmother" is a bit much.

Now if I had that much difficulty deciding how to relate to my new mother and what to call her, imagine how difficult it is for family and friends to relate to your new status as a divorced person—something that is not totally acceptable socially. Even though they may want to relate at the intellectual level, it may take them a while emotionally to get used to your new status.

The second way guilt is perpetuated is by incorrectly identifying the feeling. Perhaps you need to ask yourself, *Is it really guilt that I'm feeling, or is it the humiliation of being odd-man-out in a couple-oriented society?* Though it remains unexpressed, society's basic attitude is, "You should be married. You can only be fully functional in society and pleasing to God if you're married." Even though society is becoming increasingly aware of singles, you have lost status because of your separation or divorce, and the resulting dynamics of guilt and loss of status work hand in hand to threaten your stability. The unconscious reasoning goes, *If I had not divorced, I would not have lost status. I feel humiliated that I have assumed a lesser position in society by divorcing, and I am guilty for doing such a terrible thing to myself.*

Interestingly, a widow finds these feelings even more difficult to resolve. When her husband dies, she suffers loss of identity and feels deprived of status and rights. Often treated like a second-class citizen who will become whole again only when she remarries, she may feel guilty for being single, even though she had nothing to do with it.

It is important for you to deal with guilt constructively and be aware of the tendency to play guilt games. Narramore and Counts, in their book *Freedom From Guilt,*[4] warn against these games, which are used to keep people locked up with their guilt.

The first guilt game can be called simply "I Give Up." The person playing this game admits his guilt and assumes a posture of depression and worthlessness. The determined player won't even let the Bible speak to his need. He simply says, "I know that I shouldn't feel guilty, but . . ."

Like the game of self-pity we examined earlier, this game has several payoffs and major problems. As a growing child often discovers, parents and other significant people tend to put less pressure on someone who assumes a guilty, worthless posture. Other people who would normally remind such a person of his guilt don't bother; it's not necessary. It's also a fact that self-condemnation is easier to bear than condemnation from others. But a person playing this game must remain guilty and worthless to be "safe," thereby depriving himself of the chance for a new life with people who won't keep reminding him of his seeming guilt and worthlessness.

The second guilt game, "I'll Show You," is a rebellion against the idea of guilt. Sometimes the rebellion is active and overt; other times it's passive and covert. Whichever approach is used, the game player decides to reject anyone who makes him feel guilty. Often rejecting the established church, this person is usually marked by either active or passive hostility. By rejecting others, he closes himself off to the possibility of rich and rewarding relationships with others. Hoping to spare himself pain, he actually robs himself of the pleasure of good relationships with others.

The third guilt game, which denies wrongdoing and blames others, is called "I'm Not That Bad." This game lacks the anger and distance created in the previous game. Game players avoid bad feelings by insulating themselves with an unrealistic self-view. Often they appear to be free of guilt, but the appearance is deceiving. They wouldn't have to work so hard at rationalizing and blaming if they were as guilt-free as they pretend to be.

The problem with this type of response is that it tends to make people closed to the idea that they can do anything wrong. This perspective can lead to a totally unrealistic outlook on life and will stunt spiritual and emotional growth.

The fourth guilt game is "I'm Sorry—Please Don't Punish Me." People playing this game acknowledge their superficial faults in order to get rid of their pain. This ploy is often learned at a young age. Children discover that they can avoid spankings by quickly acknowledging their guilt. The problem with this game, however, is that its players never learn to recognize justifiable guilt and their need for restitution and change.

Well-adjusted people learn to recognize the difference between justifiable and unjustifiable guilt by facing and examining their guilt, not by avoiding it through guilt games. Open to the idea of being shown objectively where they are wrong, they are willing to offer restitution whenever possible and also confess their guilt to God.

Solution to Guilt

God offers us a marvelous solution to our feelings of guilt in 1 John 1:7. The first part of the verse, "If we walk in the light," means that when we sin, we must openly acknowledge that we have sinned. The verse goes on to include the promise that if we do this, our fellowship with God—and hopefully with our brothers and sisters in Christ—will be restored. God doesn't expect us to be perfect. But He does expect us openly to admit our mistakes.

Parents relate to their children in a similar way. If, for example, my child disobeys me and insists that he hasn't, a breach in our fellowship results. Our minds are not united on the important issue of disobedience. But when he openly acknowledges his wrong, our fellowship can be restored because our relationship is once again based on rules we agreed on.

Likewise, I don't expect my child to be asking forgiveness for wrongs that he hasn't committed. Such a response should alert me to another kind of trouble in our relationship. He may be using imagined wrongs as a way to feel safe with me, and I would have to show him that he is safe without confessing imagined wrongs.

The person who has difficulty sorting out real and imagined guilt would do well to seek professional help. He is either being victimized by a former spouse who needs to blame other people, or he himself is playing his own guilt game.

CHAPTER 8

It's the Loneliness I Can't Stand

Without a doubt, the most difficult problem you as a divorced person face is loneliness. The absence of a familiar face is only part of the story. Not only are you alone, but as a divorced person you feel socially alienated in a couple-oriented society. "I am a foreigner," one man confided to me. "Couples do their own thing. I'm left out and unwanted."

Friends and family of the divorced person should not treat his problem of loneliness lightly—as though he should be able to shake it off easily and live a happier life. I'm not writing an apologetic for loneliness, but I do think it's important that we understand the dimensions of the problem before we examine ways in which we can constructively handle it.

There are approximately 1.3 million divorced men and women in the United States below the age of thirty-five who have not remarried.[1] A high percentage of them are probably moving from person to person, hoping to find someone else to fill the lonely void left by the former spouse.

Singles apartment complexes, singles bars, and singles groups in churches are all attempts to meet one person's tremendous need for someone else. More often than not, the new relationship becomes a sexual relationship, even among churchgoing, professing Christians. The development of friendship and other characteristics of a good interpersonal relationship are often lost in a preoccupation with the sexual dimension and the resulting guilt. One divorced person, tired of a merry-go-round of sexual involvements, lamented that sex is very available on the American singles scene; friendship is not.

THE TRAUMA OF LONELINESS

Even among psychologically well-adjusted people, loneliness and alienation can produce trauma. Several years ago, experiments conducted during a "wintering over" exercise in Antarctica revealed the effects of loneliness, isolation, and alienation on scientists, military officers, and enlisted men.[2] The need for social relatedness greatly increased because of the group's isolation, and the jobs were structured to make the men interdependent.

As part of the exercise, troublesome individuals were socially censured. They were given the "silent treatment"—avoided entirely by the group. As a result, these men lapsed into what is called the "long-eye" syndrome—varying degrees of sleeplessness, crying, hallucinations, deterioration in personal hygiene, and a tendency either to move aimlessly about or to lie in bed staring blankly into space. These symptoms lasted until they were once again accepted by the group.

Not only does social alienation produce the feeling that you don't fit, but the absence of a significant other person in your life raises questions about your value as a human being. Each of us tends to depend a great deal on others for our validation as a worthwhile human being.

WAYS TO END LONELINESS

I don't pretend to have easy solutions to the problem of loneliness. In fact, I have become flatly suspicious of easy solutions, for they arise out of a failure to understand the complexity of the problem. Certainly the friendship of another person can go a long way to help ease loneliness. But in many cases, these friendships are not occurring because the people involved are missing a basic ingredient.

The irony of the search for friendships is that the answer does not lie in someone else. The starting point of all relationships is a *proper relationship with oneself.* Only when you have begun to fill your own void by enjoying your own companionship can you begin to be a good companion to someone else. The problem with frantically searching for someone else to fill your loneliness is that everyone is looking for someone else to fill the void. And when you find someone who is looking for the same thing, you're both disappointed. Neither of you can fill the void of the other because you've never learned *how to do it for yourself.*

Loneliness is most often treated as isolation from another person or group. But the dimension of loneliness that is seldom dealt with is what is happening within the lonely person. Dr. Daniel Sugarman, in *The Search for Serenity,* puts it well when he says that the person who complains about loneliness does not lack contact with people. He lacks contact with himself. When such a person makes friends with himself and enjoys his own company, he is in a better position to be a companion to someone else.[3]

The problem of loneliness usually begins in marriage and is one of the major factors in divorce. A well-balanced marriage is made up of two individuals who then function as a couple. Each individual enjoys the other and gains fulfillment in that relationship. But they also enjoy their own company as individuals. When both are experiencing a balance between their corporate and separate selves, their marriage is happy and balanced. Growing as individuals, they bring new and vital life to their relationship as a couple. The same principle applies to single and divorced people. The vitality they experience in friendship depends on the vitality they experience as single people.

People who understand and experience this vitality can make a sharp distinction between being alone and being lonely. Alone, they savor the experience of a beautiful day, a solitary walk along a path strewn with golden, autumn leaves, intense involvement in a movie, book, or play. These become very personal experiences of joy, which can later be shared with someone else.

UNDERSTAND TOGETHERNESS

A false notion of "togetherness" has contributed to the problem. True togetherness used to mean that a man and woman had to experience everything together. But more and more, people are discovering that the vitality of a relationship depends not only on what the two people experience together as a couple, but also on what they each bring to the relationship out of the experience of being *alone*.

One thing, for example, that has enriched my relationship with my wife, Fay, is what she brings to the relationship out of her solitary times. She spends much of her time reading. And when we are together, she shares with me where she has been. I haven't been there with her. But to experience through her sharing of where she has been enables me to share more of her. If she has been nowhere, if she has experienced nothing, and if she has no tastes, ambitions, desires, or dreams that are purely hers, then what does she have to offer our relationship? Such a relationship becomes a mere reflection of myself.

People who are compatible don't need to like the same things. They should mutually share some things, of course, but each can enjoy many things individually that the other can enjoy in the sharing experience. In this kind of marriage, a person is able to share his spouse's enjoyment and fulfillment even though the activity itself would not have been enjoyable or fulfilling to him.

A true friend or companion brings a part of himself—his unique experiences of life—to the relationship. This gives the other person the possibility of sharing and stretching his own experiences of life in return. So both individuals are able to enjoy life not only as individuals; they are able to share their experiences collectively.

You may say, "This means that the other person should be open to seeing life as I see it, feel it, and enjoy it—not only open to it, but willing to feel my joy." You are so right. The other person can be secure enough in himself to enjoy what he enjoys and yet share his joy with you without feeling that he must give up his interests and find joy exactly the way you do.

I am a water-sports enthusiast. Fay, on the other hand, is afraid of water because she almost drowned when she was a teen-ager. It took me a long time to understand why she was so negative whenever I talked about the fun I had sailing or surfing. Finally I realized that she was afraid that if she shared my enthusiasm, I would coax her to sail with me or drag her into the pounding surf. When I assured her that I respected her fear of the water, she no longer took away my joy by negative responses; she began to share that part of me that was very meaningful to me. Her capacity for stretching her happiness was no longer limited by her fear of the water. She could share my happiness.

An inability to share the interests of others is a large part of the problem of loneliness and the larger problem of poor interpersonal relationships. Am I secure enough to be me and still let you be you?

MAKE FRIENDS

Establish new friends by socializing. You may not feel like it, but do it. Church activities are often a good place to start. If you and your former spouse attended the same church, it may mean seeking Christian fellowship in a different circle of friends. Remember, the mutual friends you and your former spouse had may be willing to accept you both, but often they won't know how to relate to you in your new situation.

Read the newspaper for activities around town. You might attend a free concert at a local university or go to the Volunteer Fireman's Picnic even though you hate picnics. You never know whom you might meet. And if it's dull, you can go home early. Never make a decision on a social involvement that's based strictly on your feelings: chances are you won't feel like going. Again, do it!

Be as open to same-sex friendships as you would be to opposite-sex friendships. Too frequently, divorced people concentrate on opposite-sex friendships because they are look-ing for new romances. I'm not suggesting that you avoid seeking companionship with the opposite sex, but I do want to raise some warnings.

First of all, if you concentrate only on the opposite sex, you may miss the benefits of a same-sex friendship. Since there are no sexual overtones in a same-sex friendship, you open the possibility to personal growth that can be found through members of your sex. Members of your sex, particularly those in the same situation you are in, can often share helpful, objective observations about you and your situation that you may not be aware of and need to hear at this stage of your growth.

There is a temptation in an opposite-sex friendship, on the other hand, to court each other even in the first meeting. This is especially true if both people are physically and emotionally attracted to each other.

Friends of the Opposite Sex

Given the right situation, there is always the possibility of an opposite-sex friendship quickly developing into a sexual relationship outside of marriage. The formerly marrieds have built-in signals that the never-marrieds don't have. To the formerly married, the excitement of a kiss triggers the feeling "Don't stop now!" Once a person has had that feeling of letting go, it's difficult to put the brakes on.

This warning is not just addressed to religiously indifferent people. It is also meant for deeply religious people. Professing Christians are being drawn more and more into the free-and-easy-sex life style that is popularly accepted today. The attitude seems to be "Everyone else is doing it, so why can't I?"

I will say more about this trend in the chapter, "Sex, Love, and the Divorced Person." But I must share one point here. "Sex without love can make you even lonelier." This statement was made, not by someone who had a religious ax to grind, but by a woman writing in a popular feminist magazine to an audience of "liberated" women.[4] There is a growing awareness among the "sexually liberated" that the lack of a commitment in a sexual relationship leaves sex empty. This emptiness can lead to tremendous disillusionment, which in turn may make one avoid the cultivation of relationships with the opposite sex.

A woman seeking male companionship particularly runs this risk. Again and again it comes back to me through my reading and experience with my clients that many men just want to jump into bed. Since it's unlikely that this kind of man would make a good friend anyway, you haven't lost anything if he doesn't stay around after you refuse him. The only relationship that endures is based on both partners' affection, friendship, empathy, and the ability to feel self-love in that relationship.

Affection is the ability to express caring without excessive intimacy. Friendship is the ability to share common interests, tastes, and activities. Empathy is the ability to feel what that other person feels. Self-love is the ability to love one's self and feel one's self-esteem built up in the relationship. Both a man and woman need these ingredients in order to establish a meaningful relationship. If you have these in the context of commitment in marriage, sex will be good.

GIVE YOURSELF TO OTHERS

If you have been developing yourself as a person in your own right and have been learning to love yourself, then you're in a position to give yourself to others. I'm thinking in terms of voluntary activity at a church, hospital, nursing home, or some other agency that needs people who care to give themselves to the sick and the lonely. You, above all people, ought to be in a position to understand what it means to be sick, hurt, depressed, and lonely. By giving yourself to others, you will gain a measure of self-worth and take your mind off your own troubles. Sometimes the profound trouble of others makes our own trouble shrink into insignificance.

PERSONAL GROWTH GROUPS

Concerning getting involved with others, you might try attending personal growth or self-help groups. These groups are often offered in adult education programs set up by your public school system. Within each group, you will find that you can make social contact in a meaningful way, and the group may prove to be very therapeutic.

If you are a Christian, don't discount getting into a group

because the people may not be Christians. In fact, you may open yourself to a completely new dimension of growth by getting the input of people who see you first and foremost as a human being, not as a Christian.

SOLITARY REFINEMENT

If you've been developing yourself as a person, you might enjoy doing a number of activities by yourself. Terri Schultz, writing in *New Dawn* magazine, suggests the following activities.[5]

Opportunities to Read

In marriage, your time was often so consumed with family activity or meeting the needs of your former spouse that you didn't really have time for reading. Take advantage of that time now. As you discover yourself to be a more pleasant companion, go on an adventure in recreational reading. Or, if you want to do something to further your self-image, do some educational reading in a field that you've wanted to learn more about. You will discover that your reading will also make you a more interesting companion when you do make contact with others.

Physical Activity

Physical activity is an excellent way to combat depression. The very act of becoming physically active combats the malaise that goes along with depression. You may find activity enjoyable in itself (your favorite sport), or you might do it simply for the discipline (jogging or exercises). It often helps to exercise with someone else. You can keep each other involved in the program by mutual encouragement.

Perhaps you could learn a new sport. Maybe you've always wanted to learn how to play tennis, swim, or ice skate. Indulge in that impulse and learn now. Get a friend to learn with you or even teach you.

Special Meals

Whether or not you cook, you have to eat. Decide what you'd like to eat and prepare it. Even if you don't cook well and eat out a lot, take this as an opportunity to cultivate a constructive activity. Cooking will put you in touch with your tastes and desires.

Cleaning and Painting

When you have been working outside the home all day, cleaning and painting can be a refreshing change of pace. It also has other psychological benefits. Our environment can influence our mood. If it is cluttered and dingy, it can make us feel low. If it is bright and cheerful, it can lift our spirits. Such activity also gives us a sense of accomplishment.

Crafts

Your community probably has a craft shop. Go and browse, and see if anything there interests you. Often such shops also offer lessons in the various crafts they sell. These lessons are often given in groups, providing another social opportunity.

Photography

You don't need fancy gear. Whatever you have in the way of a camera will do. If you don't have one, get an inexpensive one. Then get out and take pictures. It will give you an excuse to get outside (if you need one) and will put you in touch with your aesthetic senses. We often don't know what we like or what we want to do because we've never developed a sensitivity to what pleases us. With your camera in hand, you will be looking for those things that are visibly pleasing to you.

Gardening

This may be the last thing in the world you want to do. It may seem to offer nothing but drudgery. But place this in the same category as cleaning and painting. Surroundings pleasant to the eye lift the spirit. The change seen in growing things also tends to break up the sense of sameness in one's life.

Shopping

This may seem more like a woman's thing than a man's, but if you're a man, don't pass it by. Again, we get back to what's pleasing to the eye and, in a more general sense, the development of our aesthetic sensitivities. This is a good activity, especially if you've never really developed a sense for clothes that look good on you. Taking pride in your appearance can help lift your spirits. It may draw compliments from others.

Letters and Diaries

Writing down your feelings can be tremendously therapeutic. Clients, for example, will often spontaneously write down their feelings and mail the letters to me, even though they are seeing me for weekly sessions. It helps them to express themselves and gets them in touch with their feelings. Some find that they are able to express themselves better through writing than they are through talking. A variation of this would be to call a friend on the telephone. Be careful, however, that you don't wear out your welcome by calling too often.

By getting in touch with your feelings, you will become better able to handle your heartaches and appreciate your joys. You will also find it easier to make contact with others, and your feelings of isolation will decrease in intensity.

Hibernating

Beware that you don't work too hard at combating your loneliness. Often my clients, for no apparent reason, will have bouts with crying or depression and feel that they've lost all the gains they've made. I've finally come to realize that they've been working so hard to stay on top of their loneliness that they don't indulge in even the tiniest bit of negative feelings that normally happy people sometimes experience. If you get tired of working on your loneliness, just hibernate and permit yourself to fall apart. You'll find that your tears will do you a lot of good, and giving yourself permission to take a breather from the effort will renew your desire to pick it up again.

I have not given you a cure-all for loneliness, but perhaps a beginning toward a solution. Just remember that—

- Being lonely is a natural part of being alive.
- Other people may be just a distraction from loneliness and not a cure. Some of your deepest and most painful times of

isolation came when you were living with someone you no longer felt close to. The cure for loneliness must begin with your learning to enjoy your own company.

- Loneliness is natural and not to be feared. It becomes unmanageable only when you run away from it, deny it, and treat it as an illness.

CHAPTER 9

Self-Love: The Gateway to New Relationships

Lack of self-love—self-hate—retards or prevents the development of a healthy, meaningful relationship. To develop such a relationship, you cannot begin with the relationship itself. You cannot begin with ideas on how to cultivate friendship or become more involved in activities, though these are legitimate concerns. Before you can offer anything to another relationship, you must have something to offer to yourself.

It may seem strange, but lack of self-love is at epidemic proportions in our modern society. One major reason is our cultural and Christian heritage of self-effacement. We are raised from birth with the idea that self-interest or self-love is bad and egotistical. As a result, we do everything in our power to give the message that we do not love ourselves. These games, in turn, are rewarded with the response, "Okay, since you're not loving yourself or interested in yourself, I'll love you." What an unfulfilling basis for reinforcement! No wonder people grow up with the idea that the best way to receive loving care from others is to avoid giving it to themselves.

In the Christian home, this problem becomes even more pronounced. In addition to the cultural commitment to avoid egocentricity, Christian parents who seek to maintain a commitment to biblical principles often equate normal self-love and self-interest with pride and selfishness. When their child discovers that this is the name of the game, he will look for reasons not to love himself so that he will become acceptable and loved. Most often, he will find or create a physical blemish as a reason for self-hate.

Self-hate is a mental operation that we learn. It is difficult to deal with because it is commonly viewed as an asset, not a liability. To eliminate self-hate, we must recognize its effects and make a conscious effort to love ourselves.

RECOGNIZING SELF-HATE

George Bach, in *Aggression Lab,* suggests some exercises that are designed to put you in touch with self-hate. Read through the following list of things people do to make them hate themselves and identify any of the things you do to put yourself down or to make others put you down. Here is Bach's list: "punitive shopping trips (buying ugly clothes), spending spree you can't afford (debt), working for a sadistic boss, overeating (and getting fat), promiscuity, poor partner choice (castrating women or sadistic men), getting traffic tickets, paying late taxes, mislaying important papers, living an image (intellectual, siren, etc.) and insisting on childlike and/or adolescent behavior in adult situations."[1]

Now compile your own list. What are the things you tend to do to make you hate yourself? By making a list, you discover the subtle ways you prove to yourself that you are a terrible person—a justification for self-hate.

The Effects of Self-Hate

One psychotherapist reports counseling a middle-aged woman who outshines many women half her age. Yet she insists she has physical blemishes that make her unlovable, despite the fact that no blemishes are observable. When asked if this is why her husband divorced her, she could not reply with certainty. But she is convinced she has blemishes.

It is highly unlikely that her former husband rejected her for her imagined blemishes. It is more likely that he rejected her for her own lack of self-love. Because of her imagined blemishes, she hates herself with terrible intensity. This hatred causes her to become angry at herself anytime someone pays attention to her because she feels that she doesn't deserve attention. She thinks, *If that person only knew how ugly I am, he would turn away in disgust.* Her anger, however, is interpreted by the other person as rejection, and the love that he offers is withdrawn. When the love is withdrawn, the woman then thinks, *I have been rejected because I'm ugly.*

The Benefits of Self-Hate

Why does the woman with the imagined blemishes punish herself? Somewhere, very early in life, she got the impression that she would experience less pain of rejection if she declared herself to be ugly. By anticipating rejection, she wouldn't have to look for acceptance and run the danger of being rejected by someone else. So she began to play life safe by declaring herself undesirable.

This woman's unfortunate life illustrates the importance of looking for the payoffs we seek from destructive behavior. Self-hate may be a way of establishing distance. It can also be a way to solicit love from others. How so? *Maybe if I tell others how undesirable I am, they will tell me that I'm not—something that I really need to hear.* Or, *I can use self-hate to punish others by making them feel guilty for the bad things they have done to me.* Or, *If I tell someone that I hate myself and that he is responsible, and he buys this idea, then I can really punish him and make him feel guilty when I hate myself. I may even use this in combination with one of the other payoffs. Maybe then I will get assurances that I'm not so terrible.*

HOW DO YOU LEARN TO LOVE YOURSELF?

Walter Trobisch writes that the breakthrough for a person involved in self-hate can't come from the inside. It must come from the outside. He points out that in Romans 15:7, Paul tells us that we should accept one another as Christ has accepted us.[2] *Christ has accepted us.* If only this important and necessary truth—and the many other verses of Scripture which deal with our acceptance by God in Christ—would solve the problem of self-hate. Unfortunately, a committed self-hater will always find a way to invalidate what God Himself has said by saying, "I know, but . . ." Sometimes the response is as simple as, "I know all this intellectually, but I can't feel it." And that's a good statement of the problem. The self-hater is dealing with feelings. When we are offering advice to this person, we might say, "You must walk by faith and not feelings." That's a fine principle too, but again the self-hater will say, "I know, but . . ."

Many people caught in the treadmill of self-hate will avoid pastoral counseling and Christian friends because "they don't seem to understand." The many Scripture quotations on self-love and self-acceptance[3] make the self-hater feel even more desperate and alienated. He feels that even God can't help him, because he can't translate the biblical truths he knows to be true into feelings. At this point, where can he turn?

Stop Hanging Onto Self-Hate

If you are a self-hater, you must first come to terms with your need to hang onto self-hate. You must be willing to give it up as a way to get a payoff. Again I emphasize that a psychological payoff is unconscious, not deliberate.

Assuming that the truth of your acceptance in Christ has been adequately explained, your self-hate should stop. If it still continues, more biblical study won't help. Perhaps you'll protest and say, "But according to the Bible, 'faith comes by hearing and hearing by the Word of God.'"[4] Indeed it does. But you must remove those blocks to hearing the Word.

Once you discover the payoff you're getting from self-hate, you're in a position to do something about it. You must then choose to take full responsibility for putting yourself down.

Too often self-haters act as though their bad feelings are something that overpower them. They act as though they are helpless victims. Yet, every time that you as a self-hater cultivate your self-hate by putting yourself down, *you are responsible for doing it.* Instead of saying, "I couldn't help myself," you should say, "I *didn't* help myself." There's no magic involved in this, only a basic change of attitude. You have begun to assume responsibility. You must not only maintain a responsible attitude toward self-hate, but also take the responsibility for doing something about it.

At this point, you may feel like jumping up and saying, "But what can I do? I want to start doing something now." Before we go any further, let's backtrack a moment. I want to make sure that you really understand that you are responsible for putting yourself down and that you are responsible for loving yourself.

If you are a committed self-hater, you may reply, "I know, I know! Yes, I *am* responsible for putting myself down, and that makes me hate myself even more. I'm a hopeless case!"

That phrase is a variation on the theme "I can't help myself." Are you going to take responsibility, or are you not? Are you going to try to convince yourself and others why you should hate yourself, or are you going to convince yourself why you should love yourself? Everything starts with your willingness to change.

Act on Your Commitment to Change

Once you make your decision to change, go ahead and do it, no matter how you feel about it. This principle is found again and again in the Book of Proverbs. If you do the smart thing, the rewards will follow. Proverbs urges us to do the right thing, not because we feel like it, but because it's the smart thing to do.

The same principle applies to self-love. The smart thing is to lift yourself up, not put yourself down. The smart thing is to be your own best friend, not your worst enemy. The smart thing is to do things that help build yourself up, not to do things that tear yourself down. Do you think I'm being repetitious, that I'm spending too much time on this point? Perhaps I am. But it's too important a principle to miss.

Developing self-love is difficult because every time you will start doing things to lift yourself up—being your own friend—your actions will rub you the wrong way. In fact, they will seem to precipitate a new attack of self-hate. But don't be surprised when this happens; expect it to happen. Your psychological payoff from self-hate is now threatened by your new behavior. If you keep behaving like you're okay and continue to do things that benefit your sense of self-love, you won't get your payoff—that bitter morsel that you are used to rolling around in your mouth and savoring for all of its yuckyness.

You must deliberately choose to cultivate your new attitude and behavior no matter how frequently you are tempted to engage in self-hate and destructive behavior. Accept those spontaneous, bad feelings as messages of resistance to change. Watch out that you don't use them to reinforce your game of self-hate and the "I can't help myself" attitude. Try once again to figure out what benefits you receive from indulging in self-hate. Once you know what your payoffs are, start developing self-love.

POSITIVE STEPS TO SELF-LOVE

Give Yourself Recognition

You must be doing *something* right. It doesn't matter how insignificant your accomplishment is. If you'll spend as much time thinking about the things that you're doing right as you have spent thinking about the things that you're doing wrong, you'll come up with quite a list. This takes discipline. But *do* it. Once again, though, watch out. When you start complimenting yourself, you'll be tempted to do something to counter your new experience of self-love.

It's also important to realize that even people who love themselves have moments of self-reproach. But they don't wallow in it. Don't let one incident of self-reproach convince you that you've gotten nowhere. And if you do wallow in it, realize that you're playing your old game again. Although it will be difficult, count your successes to avoid wallowing in self-reproach. You will be tempted to screen your successes out of your thinking. After all, if you start tallying up successes, you might wind up loving yourself!

Spend Time and Money on Yourself

Do the things you enjoy doing. But watch out. The commit-

/ 106

ted self-hater can turn this positive step around and use it for self-hate by thoughtlessly wasting his time and money. Give careful thought to how much time and money you're going to spend. Once you've determined what you can spend, enjoy it!

Establish Reasonable Expectations for Yourself

The words "reasonable expectations" are important here because some people program failure and resultant self-hate into their lives by placing unreasonable expectations on themselves.

Be suspicious of your failure to meet your expectations. Is this another opportunity for self-hate? Instead of concentrating on your failure, how about concentrating on the many times you have succeeded? Remember, when people think that they've done nothing good, it's probably because they don't want to see that they've done anything good.

You may say to me, "But the Bible tells us again and again how wicked we are." Indeed it does, but it also says more. If you have the tendency to hate yourself, you are in great danger of manipulating the Bible to reinforce your self-hate. Spend time reading 1 John and other passages that emphasize the total love and acceptance God gives to you as His child.

Deal With Your Anger and Self-Hate

If you are to learn to love yourself, you must also come to terms with the effects of anger on your self-hate. The person who hates himself is often angry with himself. In order to achieve self-love, you must identify what causes your anger and be willing to practice self-forgiveness. You can accomplish this through biblical meditation and inner-dialogue. George Bach offers the following inner-dialogue exercise, which will help you explore your feelings of self-hate and then conclude with self-forgiveness.[5]

1. Draw an exaggerated sketch of the ugliness you see in yourself, and use it as a dartboard.
2. Aim at the center of your shame, and express your anger at yourself as you throw the darts.
3. Exaggerate your self-hate, and caricature yourself while throwing the darts.

You may say, "You've got to be kidding. What good will that do?" I'm not kidding. Often when we exaggerate our hate, we receive relief and an emotional purging very similar to what you feel after you've been crying. When the relief comes, you usually can see things in a much better perspective. How many times, for example, have you experienced this after a good cry? Somehow things look different.

This pattern occurs over and over again in the Book of Psalms. In the first portion of a psalm, the psalmist offers a desperate cry. Then, toward the last part of a psalm, he strikes a note of optimism, almost as though light had broken through his gloom.

Two examples will illustrate this point. Psalm 3:1-2 records King David's desperate cry as he feels overwhelmed by his adversaries. In verses 3-8, David's desperation lessens. This psalm can be used therapeutically by repeating emphatically and loudly, "My adversaries have increased! Many are rising up against me! Many are saying of my soul, there is no deliverance for him in God." Shout this passage aloud with emphasis. Shout it until anger and/or tears come. Then you will be in a state of mind to read the rest of the psalm.

Do the same thing with Psalm 10. Shout it out in your own words: "Why are you hiding from me, God?" If you are angry with God, let Him know how you feel. As you are expressing your sincere anger, you will come to that place in your spirit when you will feel that God has heard you. Then you will be ready to read verses 16-18 and believe that they are true. "Thou hast heard the desire of the humble."

You might apply this methodology to the many other psalms that show this pattern. Read each psalm as though it were your experience. Read it aloud with feeling. Keep expressing your negative statements until you know that God has heard you. And if you feel that He's not hearing you, talk with Him about that. These actions are based on the same principle that Bach and other psychologists have observed and applied practically. When we emphasize a negative emotion that is difficult to get rid of, we tend to see it in better perspective and get relief from its influence.

A variation of this is to compose a psalm that addresses your own difficulties and then read it aloud to God. At first, only write about your anger or grief. Don't tell yourself that you shouldn't feel that way: the fact is that you do. Write your feelings down and read them aloud—with emphasis. When you begin to feel relief, write down your positive thoughts— about God's help or your hope for the future.

You may ask how this principle relates to positive thinking. Sometimes our positive thinking is blocked by our negative feelings. Gestalt psychologists often talk of this release in terms of "closure." If positive thinking does not work at first, then it may be that you must identify your negative feelings in order to get them out of your life. Once you get closure on them, you are ready to think positively.

This principle also relates to self-forgiveness. As we've seen, when we use self-hate exercises, we get a little better perspective on ourselves. We realize that we're not quite as bad as we make ourselves out to be. The catharsis that accompanies self-hate exercises actually releases us to forgive ourselves.

There is a great temptation not to take such exercises seriously. Clients often say, "I feel too self-conscious to do them," "They're ridiculous and won't help," or "I can't talk to God or myself in angry tones because that's a terribly unspiritual way of behaving." If you're tempted to respond like this, be careful that you're not playing a game—giving yourself an excuse to hang onto self-hate.

These are only a few suggestions, but by now you should be able to grasp that the basic principle is to *act like you love yourself*. If you run out of ideas, watch people who seem to like themselves in a normal, balanced way. What do they do to leave the impression that they feel okay about themselves? Your observations will give you other ideas of what you can do.

The regimen of loving yourself is very demanding. You should be careful that you don't become so active or continually introspective that you work yourself to exhaustion. If you love yourself, you'll give yourself a break from the effort by taking your mind off the problem from time to time.

CHAPTER 10

Sex, Love, and the Divorced Person

Sex is not just something that people do. It is also something they are—male sex/female sex. I have written this chapter with two groups of people in mind.

The first group is made up of people who have their sexual desires fairly well under control and yet are grappling with the problem of their sexual identity. Divorce often disrupts one's sense of identity, including the important aspect of sexual identity.

The second group is made up of people whose primary problem with sex is managing their sexual feelings. Despite their Christian convictions, they find themselves sorely tempted to strike up new relationships for the primary purpose of sexual involvement. As seasoned adults, they are well aware of how available sex is and how to find it.

WHAT DOES IT MEAN TO BE A MAN?

The macho male who is tough, strong, aggressive, and has many sexual conquests is on the way out. A recent survey in *Psychology Today* recorded the views of an equal number of men and women (28,000 in all) on the subject of masculinity.[1]

These people were representative of the magazine's readership.

The results surprised me. Although those surveyed tended to be less religious and more liberal than the general population, the traits they considered essential to the masculine ideal would, in many cases, receive the support of biblical Christians. For example, men listed the seven most important traits of the ideal man as follows:

1. able to love (88%)
2. stands up for beliefs (87%)
3. self-confident (86%)
4. fights to protect family (77%)
5. intelligent (71%)
6. warm (68%)
7. gentle (64%)

Last on the list of "very important" or "essential" traits was "many sexual conquests" (5%). None of the men ascribed this trait to himself.

The women surveyed tended to agree with the men on what's essential to masculinity. Here's how they ranked the seven most important traits of the ideal man (note that numbers 4 and 5 are tied with 86%):

1. able to love (96%)
2. stands up for beliefs (92%)
3. warm (89%)
4. gentle (86%)
5. self-confident (86%)
6. intelligent (84%)
7. fights to protect family (72%)

The women agreed that the top two qualities of masculinity are the ability to love and standing up for one's beliefs. The "loving" referred to here is not primarily a sexual loving, which ranks lower on the list (only 48% of the women think that being a "skilled lover" is essential to masculinity). The love the women have in mind is more reflective of the kind of love found in the Christian value system—strong in character and conviction, yet warm and gentle.

Warmth and gentleness, though valued by both sexes, are

more important indicators of masculinity to women than to men. The women agreed with the men that the least important trait is "many sexual conquests" (4%). Sexual faithfulness, on the other hand, ranked very high with the women (67%).

Many women saw an important mix of traits in the ideal man. He is strong but gentle, tough on the outside and soft on the inside, able to express emotions but not a slave to them. Here are some typical responses: "My husband treats me like a lady. . . . To the world he is assertive, self-confident, but is very able to show his fears and uncertainties to me in private." "Although my husband feels least masculine when he is home with the family, I feel the opposite. He is strong and powerful in the business world all day, but when he comes home and sometimes stays up all night nursing our sick children—the concern, gentleness, and love he shows are no less masculine."

This survey is important to men who are attempting to recover a sense of sexual identity. What *does* it mean to be masculine? Sexual conquests have virtually nothing to do with masculinity in the minds of the respondents. A real man is able to love in other ways, not merely sexually. He is also a man of character and conviction.

Jesus was not just a man; He was also masculine, a man who had the qualities of love, character, and conviction. Likewise, a divorcé suffering from a sexual identity crisis doesn't need to remarry to prove his masculinity. But he does need to be careful that he doesn't try to recapture a sense of maleness by following the macho myth and jumping in bed with the nearest available woman. As we will see, this can be more damaging than helpful. Sexual love is easy and proves nothing, while love given as an act of the will or out of the response of empathy or friendship is far more difficult to give.

The reader familiar with the above-mentioned survey may object to its use here by observing that the top seven traits listed as essential to masculinity are the same as those listed as essential to femininity. The evaluators of the survey took note of this. Many respondents expressed the humanist line that there is no such thing as masculinity or femininity—just humanity. Yet there was no single trait that readers overwhelmingly applied to men but not to women, and vice versa.

Though I am glad to see a return to the warmer, gentler qualities of masculinity, I think it's important that we don't slip into the humanist error of seeing men and women only as people and miss the differentiation between the sexes. Drs. David and Doris Jonas write about the growing incidence of impotence in males. They believe that the male population is beginning to feel a loss of differentiation between the sexes and a fusion of identity with the female.

> The male-female ideals are no longer of the old-fashioned "he-man" hero and "glamorous" enchantress types. . . . They tend to disparage competition of any kind and to prize egalitarianism in all spheres. Rather than take their places in a hierarchical social order, they tend to organize themselves into peer groups having much in common with the behavior of animals at the litter stage. . . .
>
> This brings us to what we believe to be at the root of this manifestation . . . features that are juvenile or fetal in the ancestral form. In other words, man's present form has been achieved by a series of retardations enabling him to mature sexually while still at a juvenile stage anatomically and physiologically. We see man's increasingly youthful behavior as related to this fact. . . . In the current fusion of sex roles we see a further factor in this pattern of infantilization.[2]

It would seem, then, that even though the macho image is fading, a balanced view of masculinity demands that a type of strength unique to the male persist in our thinking. This strength is seasoned with the ability to feel emotion and is not marked with the ruthlessness of years gone by.

WHAT DOES IT MEAN TO BE A WOMAN?

Women as well as men often suffer an identity crisis following divorce. The woman who is not working at the time of divorce may find it especially difficult, because she usually must alter her traditional role as mother and homemaker and seek employment. As a working woman, she will have less time and energy to fill a nurturing role with her children. She may have to let others take some of this responsibility. Nursery school or relatives may play a significant role in her children's lives.

A woman's nurturing role for the husband and family is very much a part of her idea of womanhood. Even though her former spouse may often complain, he does continue his traditional role through child support payments. But the woman's opportunity to continue her traditional role is drastically curtailed.

Another area in which a woman experiences an identity crisis is her self-image. Does she look like a woman and have womanly charms? When her husband leaves her for another woman—often a younger one—this can be especially devastating. She may use this situation constructively, by doing something about her appearance and social skills. Or, she may use it destructively to prove that men find her sexually exciting in bed.

As the *Psychology Today* survey pointed out, many of the traits considered to be essential to femininity are also considered to be essential to masculinity. Here's how the men rated the first seven traits of the ideal woman:

1. able to love (92%)
2. warm (83%)
3. stands up for beliefs (82%)
4. gentle (79%)
5. self-confident (76%)
6. fights to protect family (72%)
7. intelligent (70%)

The women rated the first seven feminine traits as follows:

1. able to love (97%)
2. stands up for beliefs (90%)
3. warm (88%)
4. self-confident (87%)
5. gentle (86%)
6. intelligent (83%)
7. fights to protect family (70%)

Traditional rumblings that broke down the "sameness of the sexes" were definitely heard beneath the egalitarian surface of the survey. In summary, the women want to rely less on marriage and children as the main criteria of femininity, while still looking up to men. Men's strength and courage were definitely valued by a number of the respondents. It seems that a corollary exists between a man who is outwardly confident and strong, while inwardly feeling gentle and warm, and the woman who is outwardly soft, while inwardly courageous and strong.

Though the characteristic of feminine softness didn't get as high a percentage of points as other characteristics, men and women both agreed that it was important (men 63%/women 62%). This softness is not to be confused with the fainting phenomenon of the Victorian era or with the dumb blonde of the forties and fifties. Nor is it to be confused with manipulatively dependent women who play their games with men in every era. It is a softness that says to the man, "You have something special to offer me in your physical and emotional strength." It is a softness of appearance (skin, hair, clothing), of voice, and of manner.

In the past ten or twenty years, the move toward a more egalitarian society has tended to shift the focus off the softness of women. The following changes are significant: more pants and fewer dresses; less make-up; in many cases, de-emphasis of the female breast; and an almost pathological disavowal of what was once considered feminine beauty. These changes, of course, have accompanied the attempt to consider women primarily as people and not as sex objects.

Despite this trend, definite distinctions between women and men remain. Underscoring a woman's softness in manner and appearance as one of her distinguishing characteristics does have validity. Though the chauvinism of Shakespeare's *Taming of the Shrew* may be outdated, the bard's observations about the softness of the female body speak of a view that will not die.[3]

During the 1976-77 television season, Farrah Fawcett-Majors was the current woman among women. Two million copies of her picture poster sold in only four months. What special qualities does Farrah possess? No one seems to agree, even psychiatrists. Regardless of their different explanations, people seeking to understand the reasons behind her success seem to agree that the American public is trying to recapture the feminine softness that was lost in the unisex insanity of the sixties without going back to the demeaning "dumb blonde" image of the forties and fifties. Farrah's softness is not just in appearance; it carries over in her manner and voice as well.

Mannerisms and the way a woman carries herself are important. If certain mannerisms and prissy gestures by men are considered unmasculine to women, then certain gestures and mannerisms in women are in the same way unfeminine to men. Men still have definite ideas of what a lady should be. She must carry herself and sit with grace. Her speech and manner must not be coarse. Though coarseness is not appreciated in men, it is less accepted in women. Girls are still reared to be "prim and proper."

I do not underrate the important inner qualities women should possess that I described earlier in this chapter. Inner strength is important to the woman who would make it successfully as a divorcee. She must learn to cope with the outside world that her former husband may have coped with for her. But if she can retain her softness and her nurturing spirit for her children, she will retain the essential characteristics of femininity.

UNDERSTANDING YOUR SEXUAL VULNERABILITY

Men and women each have their particular sexual vulnerability. I will be brief on the subject; other books address themselves entirely to the subject of sexuality.[4] Understand, also, that I'm generalizing on male and female sexuality, since individual differences in particular personalities don't always follow the general pattern. But I think it's important to think in this direction.

Female Sexual Vulnerability

If you are a woman and have been disappointed in marriage, you might think that this part of the book is not for you. You may feel that you've had it with men. Or, you may feel that you're safe, because you've lost your interest in sex. Yet it is important for you to realize that you are still sexually vulnerable.

/ 117

Because of her sexual complexity, a woman may be more sexually vulnerable in some respects than a man. Dr. Marc H. Hollender reports that the main sexual aim of some women is to be held. They desire closeness and even physical contact, but do not feel "sexual" about it. In short, they seek "cuddling" as an end in itself.[5]

Many women who enjoy both coitus and cuddling can separate the two desires in their thinking. What makes them vulnerable is that the two are inseparably bound together. For example, a woman may begin an evening with her date with only cuddling on her mind, but suddenly find herself going beyond that point, either because of a surprising change in her feelings or because she wants cuddling so badly that she will exchange sex for it.

Dr. Hollender says that a woman will frequently use sexual excitement to get a man to hold her.[6] He says further that the craving to be held sometimes explains promiscuity. Sex is bartered. The woman gives the man what he desires (coitus); in return, he gives her what she wants (cuddling).

A woman is a sexually defensive creature. She is not aroused easily. Before she permits herself to become sexually involved with a man, she must feel valued by him as a person. This happens when the man treats her with deference and respect and touches her in a nonsexual way that communicates, "You're nice to be with."

Though a woman is sexually defensive and needs a feeling of security with a man ("He wants *me*, not my body"), her need for security can actually work against her. She may imagine a greater degree of security with the man than there really is. A worldly-wise man can then take advantage of her. This is what the art of seduction is all about. The man creates a climate for sexuality by avoiding sexual overtures and making the woman feel like a special person. When he holds her, he satisfies her craving to be held and does not alarm her by getting sexual. When such a woman has not been held by a caring man in a long time and has had doubts about anybody's caring, her defenses quickly vanish.

Dr. Hollender points out that tactile stimulation serves

much the same purpose sexually for women as visual stimulation does for men.[7] A woman's desire to be held may have no conscious sexual overtones. But a rush of sexual feelings might come quite unexpectedly when she is held.

I don't want to portray men as seducers of women. But the worldly-wise man is going to do what comes natural to him. When he is aware that the woman is disarmed, he will make some tentative sexual moves. And even though she recognizes that they are sexual moves, she has been disarmed. She is persuaded that he is not just after her body. And fantasizing a high degree of security with him, she may think, *Why not? I really feel married to him. I am somebody special to him.* Although she may be special to him, is she special enough to him to surrender sexually to him? Her need to be held, her desire to demonstrate her caring for him, and her own sexual feelings all conspire to make her surrender.

Vulnerability does not mean a woman should steer clear of men. I am only pointing out *vulnerability*. The better a woman understands her sexuality, the better she can handle opposite-sex friendships and dates when they come along. When she has that craving to be held, she will be aware of what it's about. When she is tempted to fantasize about her security with a man, she will be aware that there is a difference between her desire to feel secure and special to him and the reality of the situation. Divorced women quickly discover that divorce laws don't guarantee the permanence of a relationship. But the prospect of marriage has a way of separating the honorable from the dishonorable. A contract has a way of separating those who shop around from those who are ready to buy.

A tragic story that graphically reveals the differences between male and female sexuality is the story of the rape of Tamar in the Bible.[8] Amnon "loved" her with such a passion that he pretended to be ill in order to make sexual advances toward her. She resisted his advances. So he raped her and then threw her out. She was outraged, for he had treated her as a thing, not as a person. Even though he had forced himself on her and she had resisted him, in her mind he *owed* her something. I don't mean "owing" in the sense of paying a common prostitute for her services. Amnon had violated far more than Tamar's body; he had also wounded her spirit. Women attach relationship and obligation to their sexuality. Watch out that you're not misled. Does he want "it," or does he want you?

MALE SEXUAL VULNERABILITY

Just as a woman tends to be a sexually defensive person, a man tends to be sexually aggressive and is easily aroused. The arousal of a male occurs through a subtle combination of physiological and psychological forces, but the normal male is well aware of two things. First, he is easily aroused by what he sees. Second, the longer the period of sexual abstinence, the more sexual he feels and the more easily aroused he is by what he sees. The human male is designed so that the pressure of his sexual feelings is eventually released through ejaculation. This occurs either by his choice (intercourse or masturbation) or spontaneously through a wet dream. The dream is accompanied by sexual feelings.

His vulnerability is further heightened by dress styles and pictorial displays that make the female body sexually appealing. Availability of easy sex further heightens his vulnerability, since he can make some sexual distinctions too. Like most men, he is aware of purely sexual feelings devoid of any personal, emotional warmth. He feels that he can have sexual relations without having any feelings for the woman as a person. This is not to say that he won't pay a price for this kind of encounter, because he will. What I am saying is that his readiness for sex as an end in itself, and its blatant availability, makes him very vulnerable.

This does not contradict what I said about a woman and her sexuality. *She* may not think that sexual relations are an end in themselves for the man. Although few men would say so directly, many think, *Why buy the store when you can get all the goods you want free?*

The male's capacity to distinguish between purely sexual feelings and those that result from commitment to a person partly explains the phenomenon of prostitution. Male prostitution (except for the homosexual variety) is far less common than female prostitution. Females just don't seek out male prostitutes. They look for more than sex. They look for some kind of relationship, though it may be short-lived.

Men, on the other hand, will gratify themselves sexually and feel that the relationship is over after paying for it. In return, the female prostitute has received what she wants—her pay. Sexually gratified prostitutes are a myth. If prostitutes receive any gratification at all, it is found in their contempt for the men.

It may appear that the male's sexual vulnerability is fairly uncomplicated. And in many senses it is. But what usually isn't discussed is what goes on in the male's mind in terms of rationalizations and devious plans to fulfill himself sexually. A man with scruples just doesn't go out and find a woman. He rationalizes himself into a sexual encounter. Jesus referred to this type of rationalization when He said:

> You have heard that it was said, "you shall not commit adultery"; but I say to you, that every one who looks on a woman to lust for her has committed adultery with her already in his heart.[9]

This passage is often taken to mean that lusting in one's heart is as bad as the actual act. If this is the case, why shouldn't the person go ahead with the act, since he's already indicted? The context in which Jesus was talking answers this question. In the surrounding verses, Jesus describes a number of sinful acts that take place because they were permitted to find a place in our hearts. Murder, for example, finds its origin in unresolved anger. Adultery, likewise, finds its origin in unresolved lust. A man sees an attractive, available woman—what does he think? Does he toy with the idea of getting into bed with her? Does he fantasize about how great she'd be in bed? Women also fantasize, but their fantasies generally (certainly not always) accompany the idea for some kind of a relationship with the man.

I stress the danger of fantasy to the divorcé because it's a fact of life that you are going to be easily turned on sexually. You experienced it before marriage, and now with what you know, the turn-ons are all the more obvious. What are you going to do with that turn-on? Your natural temptation will be to fantasize a sexual involvement.

Sex, Love, and the Divorced Person

With the female's orientation being basically one of relationship and the male's orientation being basically one of sexuality, you can see why the word *love* confuses so many people. When a man or a woman says, "I love you," what does he or she mean? Most likely feelings of companionship and the admiration of the man's personal characteristics are the paramount elements of the woman's feeling. Most likely the sexual attraction is the paramount element of the man's feeling. I don't mean to say that men are completely devoid of other emotions and needs and that women are devoid of sexual feelings of attraction. Indeed, women will protest this belief as loudly as men! What I am trying to point out, however, is that many divorced people are very confused about love.

Types of Love

Several types of love are readily seen in male/female relationships. Psychologist Everett Shostrom has developed a test called "The Caring Relationship Inventory" in which seven types of love are evaluated.[10] He defines these loves as follows:

Affection is a helping, nurturing form of love. It involves unconditional giving and acceptance of another person as characterized by the love of a parent for a child.

Friendship is a peer love based on appreciation of common interests and carries a respect for each other's equality.

Eros is a possessive, romantic form of love, which includes features such as inquisitiveness, jealousy, and exclusiveness. It often has an exploitive bent, loving the other for what that person can do for oneself.

Empathy is a charitable, altruistic form of love that feels deeply for the other individual as another unique human being. It involves compassion, appreciation, and tolerance.

Self-love is the ability to accept in a relationship with another person one's weaknesses, as well as to appreciate one's individual, unique sense of personal worth. It includes the acceptance of one's full range of positive and negative feelings toward the other person in the relationship. Or, to put it another way, is it possible to love yourself in this relationship or does that other person make you feel less than worthwhile?

Besides those five types of love, Shostrom adds the following two subtypes to his test:

Being-love is the ability to accept the other person as he or she is. It includes aspects of loving the other person for the good you see in him. It is an admiring, respectful love, an end in itself.

Deficiency-love is the love for another person which is based on what he can do for you. It is an exploitive, manipulative love that is a means to an end. Almost half of the items included under erotic love are also included in this subtype.

In Western society, practically all love relationships begin with erotic love. It is the romantic form of love that people are said to fall into—"we have fallen in love." It is thought to be quite beyond our control, and otherwise unacceptable behavior is often excused when a person is smitten with this condition.

Although it's true that some relationships based on friendship grow into romantic love, few people today marry a mere friend. Their love usually starts with an attraction to the other person's appearance and personality. Even though the person might not be physically attractive, his personality may be the attractive element.

The divorced person runs the risk of jumping into this romantic type of relationship. After being starved for all those good feelings for so long and suddenly feeling so good with a person, the divorced person tends to take leave of his senses. People have said to me, "But we have more than just a physical attraction for each other. All those other forms of love exist too." I don't doubt the sincerity of those people. But knowing how romantic love makes us fantasize, I doubt that a person "in love" is really being objective.

By itself, romantic love can be extremely dangerous. The person loved tries to maintain the image for which he is loved, but over the long haul, that image will tarnish. Likewise, the one loving tends to live in a fantasy world where the loved one is always handsome and charming and can do no wrong. When Prince or Princess Charming does reveal his/her uglier side, the ugliness is excused or overlooked.

Erotic love generates lots of good feelings, which are often the sole basis for marriage. After the ceremony, disillusionment sets in. No one can live with a person twenty-four hours a day, seven days a week, and keep him on a pedestal. Slowly but surely, the real person will emerge from the fantasy and the importance feelings played in the relationship will lessen dramatically.

What happens when the dream goes "poof"? What happens when those traits, habits, mannerisms, tastes, and values that you considered of no consequence now seem intolerable? Gradually those good feelings that you had when you "fell in love" disappear, and you find yourself "falling out of love."

Erotic love does not offer an adequate foundation for marriage, though it is certainly an important element. The emphasis that American society has placed on feelings has excluded other important types of love. Will these other types remain when *eros* fades? The answer to that question depends on a type of love not yet mentioned: volitional love—love as an act of the will.

The Bible calls volitional love *agape* love. Volitional love doesn't depend on one's feelings, nor does it depend on the attractiveness or worth of the person loved. It rises purely out of one's own decision to love; it is a matter of choice.

As the most noble form of love there is, volitional love is the love that God had when He *chose* to send His Son, Jesus Christ, to die on the cross for the satisfaction of our sins. The Bible makes it clear that God didn't find us lovely. But it also stresses the fact that even though we are sinners, Christ died for us. We didn't first love God, prompting Him to respond to us. Rather, He demonstrated true love by loving us and sending His Son to die for our sins. This kind of love also brings a response. Again, the Bible says that we love God because He first loved us.[11]

Let's apply this truth to male/female relationships. Affection, friendship, empathy self-love, and being-love can all be exercised as an act of the will. You don't need to feel good about another person to demonstrate this kind of love. And when you *choose* to love like this, you run the best chance of generating a reciprocal love that will in turn generate good feelings.

I can choose to be affectionate, to give unconditionally to you, and to accept you. I can choose to be a friend, to respect your equality and learn to like the things you like. I can choose to love empathetically, to have compassion, appreciation, and tolerance. I can choose to love myself in our relationship, to accept my weaknesses and strengths. I can choose to love you as you are, to respect you for who you are and not for what I can get out of my love relationship with you.

First Corinthians 13 describes *agape* love. This type of love is patient, kind, not jealous, does not brag, is not arrogant, does not act rudely, is not self-seeking, is not easily provoked, does not keep score of wrongs suffered, is not glad when someone else commits sin, bears all types of difficulties, and has unlimited faith, hope, and endurance.

You may be thinking, *These principles are good and should be practiced. But no doubt you can practice them easier than I can. If I grow to love someone, he could tax my love twenty-four hours a day.* You're right; *agape* love isn't always easy to apply. But here's where you have another choice to make—a fundamental choice. Stripping away all the fantasies of romantic love, you must determine what it's going to cost to love that other person. This kind of intelligent choice begins a lasting relationship; the ongoing choice to love will help to keep the relationship going. For example, does the relationship have so many barbs or rough edges that loving means that you will have to endure constant pain?

It may seem strange to address this subject to divorced people, but they run the same risk with romantic love that teen-agers do. They can easily be deluded by romantic love and get involved in a new relationship by "falling in love" rather than by intelligent choice.

The notion of romantic love is relatively new in the history of man. For most of our history, marriages were arranged. Those who arranged the marriages felt that, given the right circum-

/ 125

stances for a good marriage, the feelings would come later. And an examination of history will reveal that their system was no worse and generated no more unhappiness than our romantic love today.

I'm not advocating a return to arranged marriages. But there is certainly a place in relationships for the feelings and will to operate together. As Rollo May points out in *Love and Will*, the hippies rebelled against the assembly-line, sex-on-Saturday-night artificiality of bourgeois love and stressed the immediacy of erotic love. But that extreme must be balanced by an act of the will. The will must take those good feelings and mold them into fidelity and lasting love.

HANDLING YOUR SEXUAL FEELINGS

The availability of sex in America today is no secret. As a divorced person, you will soon discover—if you haven't already—how openly members of the opposite sex will convey to you their sexual availability. This goes for the married, divorced, and widowed. Even a church environment is no protection. Though it is covert, sexual permissiveness in many churches is approaching Corinthian proportions. The stigma of the Scarlet Letter no longer exists. Even though the Bible clearly states that intercourse outside of marriage is a sin, social restraints are weak or nonexistent. The church is forced to carry the social (as well as biblical) ban by itself, but is finding this position more and more difficult to enforce.

If you are jaded by the many warnings and prohibitions you have heard preached from the pulpit, listen to those who have had sexual relations outside of marriage.

An eighteen-year-old girl, describing her first sexual experience, said to me bitterly, "All my friends told me how great it was—that they were making love with their boyfriends all the time and it was terrific. So I tried it. It was nothing but a big disappointment. I felt used."

In a feminist magazine article titled, "Why Two People End Up Lonely, Bitter—Even in a Double Bed," a woman argues that good sex is not enough. Or, to put it another way, she asks the question, "Is there life after orgasm?" and then concludes that "commitment and long-term interests" are essential to a good sexual relationship.[12] This position is startling: a "liberated" woman writing about "the new woman and the new man" is still using such "old-fashioned" words as "commitment" and "long-term interests." Her final description of sex without commitment is extremely powerful. "We feel vaguely betrayed," she writes, "as if we sacrificed our integrity for security and a warm bed."[13]

A woman writing in another feminist magazine attempts a mildly humorous treatment of sex by asking the question, "Who Ever Said Sex Is Fun?" But she doesn't seem amused when she writes, "It's not the actual sex act I hated. It's the side effects, the surprises that go along with the instant intimacy of intercourse." Nor does she sound too humorous when she says, "I hate the morning after. You're hoping he doesn't mind that your mouth tastes like a dirty ashtray, and he's wishing he could nail you once more without having to talk."[14]

These "liberated" women have no religious ax to grind. Yet, in the laboratory of life, they have learned an important lesson about interpersonal relationships. Casual sex is not all it's cracked up to be.

Late one afternoon, a Christian colleague and I were discussing the many tragic cases we have handled as a result of people experimenting with sex outside of marriage. During our conversation, he said something startling, yet understandable. "My Christian love for my wife and my convictions have always made me faithful to my wife. But," he continued, "after working with so many people who say that sex without the commitment of marriage is tragic, I'm a greater believer in fidelity than ever before!"

"Okay," you may say, "you've made your point. But what do I do with my sexual feelings? You've already said that a person shouldn't jump right into a new marriage. So where does that leave me?"

That's a fair question. But let me handle it in two different situations you will face: dating, and when you are alone.

In a Dating Situation

When you begin to date again, you must do what you probably did when you were a teen-ager—set the limits on how far you're going to go. But as a divorced person, this decision is even more imperative. As a sexually aware person who knows his way around, you're more likely than a teen-ager to take some short-cuts to heavy sexual involvement. Larry Richards's book *How Far Can I Go?* (Moody Press) is excellent on this subject, even though it was written for teen-agers.

Several principles may help you to avoid going too far.

First, avoid compromising situations where you might have intercourse without fear of discovery. Meeting in an apartment, parking in a car in a lonely place, or being alone in parks or wooded areas away from public view are examples of compromising situations.

Second, avoid overexposure. When you find that your thoughts are constantly occupied by your date and that you constantly must be in touch with him, watch out. Physical distance is still the best way to cool a hot relationship. Joseph, the son of Jacob, chose this situation when he ran from Potiphar's wife,[15] and the apostle Paul advised it when he told Timothy to "flee youthful lusts."[16] You don't suddenly fall into a sexual relationship with another person. It's the result of a lot of fantasizing and scheming to find ways to get close.

Third, avoid alcoholic beverages. Alcohol lowers inhibitions. When your inhibitions are already strained to the breaking point, you don't need a drink to push you over the brink.

Fourth, plan your activities carefully in advance. It's unlikely that you'll wind up in a compromising situation if you make definite plans. If you're a woman and your date doesn't have any definite plans, make some suggestions.

Fifth, select your dates with care. As a mature adult, you know who's on the make and who isn't. Don't kid yourself that big boys or big girls don't get burned when they play with fire.

Sixth, avoid activities that are overly stimulating. Movies and literature heavy with sexual themes or activities that offer a lot of body contact will encourage sexual involvement.

Seventh, develop a positive mental attitude about the virtues and practical value of reserving sex for marriage. Remember, your biggest problem with handling your sexual feelings is with what goes on between your ears. You are what you think. If you think that God is a spoilsport for restricting sexual intercourse to marriage and you find it difficult to apply that principle by faith, then learn from the experience of others who have ended up lonely and bitter in a double bed.

Alone With Your Sexual Feelings

Dealing with sexual feelings in a dating situation is only part of the problem. What should you do when you're alone and get those feelings that start your mind to scheming?

First, recognize that sexual feelings are vitally related to physical energy—like a boiler with a head of steam. It often helps to bleed off that energy with vigorous physical activity. You'd be surprised how a couple of hours of handball or tennis can take the edge off. Sure, it takes discipline. But disciplined people are the ones who enjoy the rewards of life.

Second, recognize that sex is also a state of mind. If you are preoccupied with thoughts of sex, they can be sublimated. You can get your mind off sex and onto something else by involving yourself in an activity that calls for other uses of your brain and emotions.

In his book, *Sexual Understanding Before Marriage*, Herbert Miles suggests that involvement in the lives of children or the aged is often an excellent way to put your emotional energies to good use. Emotional involvement, he believes, has the same effect in expending surplus emotional energy that physical exercise has on physical energy.[17]

Third, use aversive therapy on yourself. Aversive therapy follows the principle of creating a negative image of an otherwise attractive idea. In this case, whenever you are tempted to fantasize sexual involvement with an attractive, available person, think of the disastrous consequences instead. You may, for example, feel vaguely betrayed, as if you have "sacrificed your integrity for security and a warm bed." Instead of feeding your feelings with pornographic magazines or movies, choose to read about people who have experimented with sex outside of marriage and found it to be a bad experience.

What About Masturbation?

We can't leave the subject of handling sexual feelings without considering the subject of masturbation. Is masturbation a legitimate way to prevent sexual intercourse outside of marriage, or is it just the substitution of one problem for another?

Christian literature has been more open about the subject in recent years, although many different views have been expressed. Opinions on the subject range from the declaration that it's "a gift of God" to the belief that it's absolutely sinful.

Charlie Shedd considers masturbation a gift of God which can be used for either good or evil. He says that it prevents situations from getting out of hand, but should not be allowed to become compulsive. He also cautions against perverted or twisted thoughts arising from masturbation that are harmful to oneself or others.[18]

Cecil Osborne agrees with Shedd in *The Art of Learning to Love Yourself*. He sees "absolutely nothing wrong with masturbation" and speaks of the damage done by parents who utter the grave words to their children, "Don't touch yourself down there."[19]

Shirley Rice approaches the subject in the context of marriage. She says that since masturbation is not mentioned in the Bible and there is no scientific evidence to show that it's harmful, except in excess, the only wrong is in lustful thoughts or extreme self-centeredness. Other Christian counselors taking the same point of view suggest that if the fantasy is for one's spouse, then it isn't wrong. Rice does make it clear, however, that masturbation is only a temporary expedient in marriage and not a solution.[20] Adequate sexual relations should be the goal—not a private, individual orgasm.

Walter and Ingrid Trobisch engage in a lengthy correspondence on the subject of masturbation, writing to a young woman named Ilona in *My Beautiful Feeling*.[21] They take a nonjudgmental viewpoint and suggest that there is a difference between using masturbation as an emergency measure and falling into a regular habit or addiction. They suggest to Ilona that everyone has to decide for himself. The correspondence also reveals a psychology that tends to make Ilona relax and be less preoccupied with masturbation. This, in turn, seems to take away the importance Ilona had placed on it and gives her the opportunity to confess whatever guilt she might have developed.

Herbert Miles offers further insight on the subject of masturbation when he suggests that masturbation may be used by the male to avoid sexual immorality. He takes the position that the physiology of the male ultimately demands ejaculation for the release of semen and the accompanying release of sexual desire, whether it results from a wet dream, masturbation, or intercourse. Miles holds that the male who is unable to wait for a wet dream may have to resort to masturbation to avoid immorality.

Miles does believe that masturbation is sinful when (1) it is used for sheer pleasure; (2) it becomes compulsive; and (3) it results in guilt feelings.[22] He feels that it is not sinful when it is limited and temporary.

Dr. Miles opposes masturbation for women, however. He argues that since the female sex drive does not demand release through masturbation, its use would be merely for pleasure and not because of demand, as in the case of the male. Some women have found this position to be discriminatory. They maintain that their need for release is just as urgent as the males'.

Perhaps the greatest debate on the subject focuses on the fantasy that accompanies masturbation. Some argue that it's impossible to masturbate without the fantasy being a sin. Others maintain that if the fantasy is for one's former spouse, the fantasy is not sinful. Still others claim the act can be performed simply as an act of release without fantasizing.

Probably there is disagreement because we are dealing with a "doubtful" or "debatable" issue. The foregoing discussion shows that some Christian writers do not categorically dismiss masturbation as sin. The Bible is silent on the subject, with the exception of its condemnation of lustful fantasy. The inter-

/ 131

pretative rule in such a case is to permit each Christian to decide the issue for himself. The apostle Paul followed this principle on the issues of eating meat offered to idols and the observance of holy days.[23] Paul's guidelines are (1) will it hurt me? (2) will my example hurt the weaker brother? and (3) will it hurt my testimony before others?

Trobisch comes closest to applying this principle when he writes:

> Everyone has to decide for himself. No one is allowed to judge the other one and no one can decide for him. If you want to walk on the tightrope, you have to take the responsibility for yourself. We are not the lords of your conscience. It is the Holy Spirit who alone has to tell you in each situation whether you can have a good conscience or not.[24]

CHAPTER 11

Remarriage and the Bible

Three out of four divorced people marry again,[1] and many of these people believe that remarriage is a necessity. Stanley A. Ellisen writes:

> The option of remarriage may not be just a right; it may be a responsibility. It may constitute a physical and spiritual necessity. To see it as a mere right which one may or may not claim falls short of the Bible's overall revelation on marriage and the redemption God provides in Christ. . . . The provision of remarriage must be seen as more than a right to be conceded. It is a positive good to be pursued, when done according to the principles God gave.[2]

This chapter will examine the subject of remarriage from the biblical standpoint. In the next chapter, we'll look at some practical considerations of remarriage.

In chapter 2, I outlined two approaches to divorce: (1) divorce without remarriage, though not God's ideal, is not a sin; and (2) if divorce is a sin, it is forgivable and a redemptive attitude ought to prevail.

Once again we must consider the words of Moses, Jesus, and Paul, this time addressing the question of remarriage.

/ 133

MOSES ON REMARRIAGE

In Deuteronomy 24:1-4, the law of Moses provided that a divorced woman could remarry. This position indicates that divorce dissolves a marriage and is not merely separation. The only remarriage banned under the law was a woman's remarriage to a former husband after she had remarried and divorced. The example given is a case where a woman divorced, remarried, and divorced again. When she was divorced or widowed by her second husband, she could not return to the first one. But the law did allow her to take a third husband.

As we noted in chapter 4, two schools of thought developed on this subject. The liberal school of Hillel permitted divorce and remarriage on any ground, while the conservative school of Shammai permitted divorce and remarriage only on the ground of infideltiy. In this historic context, Jesus spoke on the subject.

JESUS ON REMARRIAGE

Jesus' words on remarriage are recorded in Matthew 5:32; 19:3-12; Mark 10:11-12; and Luke 16:18. I will examine only the Matthew 19 passage, since it is the most comprehensive and is also the most widely debated—particularly on the question of remarriage.

When the Pharisees began questioning Jesus about His position on divorce and remarriage, He went back to the original concept of marriage given in Eden. There was to be no divorce and remarriage. Jesus went on to point out, however, that God permitted divorce and remarriage under the Mosaic law "for your hardness of heart."[3] This phrase is generally interpreted to mean that sin's entrance into the world prompted God to alter His original pattern.

Jesus then uttered His controversial words. "And I say to you, whoever divorces his wife, except for immorality, and marries another commits adultery" (Matt. 19:9). The debate on this verse stems from the exception clause—"except for immorality." Although the Greek word for "immorality," *porneia*, has a wider definition than the word for adultery, it includes adultery.

What does this exception mean? A number of interpretations have been offered. The Roman Catholic Church sees the exception as offering no ground at all for remarriage. Some Protestant scholars have taken the position that *porneia* refers to the marriage of an individual to a close blood relative (consanguineous marriage) rather than to adultery. They maintain that if Jesus were permitting divorce and remarriage on the ground of adultery, He would have been agreeing with the conservative school of Shammai—something they maintain He did not intend to do. The amazed response of the apostles (v. 10), they add, further supports this view. They say that the disciples understood that divorce and remarriage were possible only if someone had married a close blood relative. Still others argue that the word *porneia* refers to sexual immorality—which includes adultery—rather than to consanguineous marriage. Traditionally, Protestants have held the view that Jesus was granting permission to divorce and remarry on the ground of infidelity by one's spouse. *Porneia* is then understood to mean adultery.

PAUL ON REMARRIAGE

The apostle Paul gives us another line of evidence to consider in 1 Corinthians 7:10-15. The traditional interpretation of this passage is that divorce and remarriage are permitted on the ground of desertion. But this interpretation has been challenged by others, who argue that the statement of not being under bondage (v. 15) does not conclusively teach freedom from the marriage. It is argued further that if Paul were permitting divorce and remarriage on the ground of desertion, then he would be contradicting Jesus' statement that there is only one ground: adultery.

TRADITIONAL VIEWS OF REMARRIAGE

In my opinion, these latter arguments about Paul's writings are invalid because the challengers do not understand that Jesus and Paul are dealing with two separate, traditional categories of marriage. Jesus, dealing with *Christian* marriage, permits remarriage on the ground of sexual immorality alone. Paul, on the other hand, is dealing with the marriage of a *believer and unbeliever*, in which the unbeliever may not want to remain in the marriage. In that particular case, desertion is permitted as a ground for divorce. Biblically, then, adultery is the only valid ground for remarriage for the Christian, and Paul does not challenge that fact.

Since the Reformation, Protestant churches have traditionally held to three grounds for remarriage: adultery, desertion, and cruelty. Cruelty is included because it is considered to be a form of "constructive desertion." A spouse may behave so badly, in other words, that a parting of the ways is unavoidable.

CONTEMPORARY VIEW OF REMARRIAGE

Meanwhile, in our modern age, marital battles continue. It doesn't matter what the church says: husbands and wives divorce and remarry anyway. Christians, no longer bystanders, in many instances ignore the traditional views and remarry. They can't wait for scholars to come up with a uniform opinion that will be true both to Scripture and to the realities of life. This growing trend has exerted tremendous pressure on evangelical churches to rethink the entire issue, to find some way to handle its remarried and remarrying Christian constituency.

Dr. George Ensworth, professor of pastoral psychology at Gordon-Conwell Theological Seminary, reviewed the new trends of thinking in the June 1976 issue of *Eternity* magazine.[4] In his article, he placed Guy Duty at one end of the spectrum. Duty holds out for the traditional view of divorce and remarriage on the ground of adultery or desertion alone.[5] At the other end, Ensworth placed Dwight Small, who advances the idea that "there is a progress of ethical saying applied to all; not every ethical declaration can be universalized."[6]

Small propounds the view that three ages of ethical administration are seen: (1) the Mosaic Period of the Old Testament, where God exercised his conditional will because of the hardness of the heart and lack of the indwelling Holy Spirit; (2) the Future Kingdom Period, in which righteousness will be perfectly fulfilled; and (3) the Interim Church Period, the present, which is administered under grace rather than law.[7]

Dr. Small further concludes that Christ's ban on divorce and remarriage except on the ground of adultery is a commandment for the Kingdom Period, not the Interim Church Period in which we live. He believes that marriage should be honored, but that the ideals Christ laid out should not be rigorously applied to this sinful age. Since the Christian who fails at marriage lives under grace, Small writes, the forgiveness of God enables him to start again, even in a new marriage.[8]

Small's approach seems to relieve us of many problems surrounding the question of remarriage. He offers us a way to hold to the literalness of Jesus' teaching without feeling bound to an unworkable marriage. But this view has been criticized too. Some Christians believe that serious compromises will be made if Christ's words are taken as an ideal for the Kingdom Period and not as principles to be rigorously applied to the Interim Church Period of grace. They argue that if other ethical teachings of Christ are handled in the same way, Christ's teachings could become irrelevant for our present age. Still others believe that Christ was not speaking of the Kingdom Period, but rather of our present age.

Ensworth's final summary reflects a position taken by many evangelical writers today.

> First, God's intention in creating mankind male and female and in ordaining marriage is clear. Human sexuality finds fulfillment in marriage, and marriage is a permanent and exclusive union. This is the divine purpose and ideal. Second, divorce is nowhere commanded or even encouraged in Scripture. Third, nevertheless, divorce (and remarriage) is permissible on two grounds. First, an innocent person may divorce his/her partner if the latter has been guilty of immorality. Secondly, a believer may acquiesce in the desertion of his/her unbelieving partner, if the latter refuses to go on living with him/her. In both cases, however, permission is granted in negative (that is reluctant) terms: only if a person divorces his partner on the ground of unchastity is he not committing adultery. Only if the unbeliever insists on departing is the believer "not bound."[9]

Remarriage and the Redemptive Attitude

Toward the conclusion of his article, Dr. Ensworth issues a call to be true to Scripture and yet remain compassionate toward those who fail at marriage and try again. He writes:

> We dare not compromise nor water down the clear teaching of Scripture before the fact, nor dare we withhold the understanding and forgiveness and renewal of the Gospel of grace after the fact. . . . But that in applying that principle to the individual situation, we counsel in pastoral care to help each new marriage in responsible commitment. The church can minister redemptively and respond with healing grace without denying the judgment of law concerning marital commitment. Thus the individual may find restoration to full fellowship and ministry in the life of the church.[10]

The sinfulness of divorce *without* remarriage on grounds other than adultery might be questioned, as I have done in chapter 4. But there is little doubt that remarriage on any other ground is sinful. Despite this fact, the redemptive approach to remarriage described by Ensworth in the above quotation may offer us the possibility of being true to Scripture on one hand, and dealing with the realities of life on the other. The approach can be applied both before and after divorce and remarriage take place and enables separated or divorced people to find a place in Christian fellowship and the church.

Someone may say, "It's easy enough to exercise a redemptive attitude after remarriage has taken place. If a person has already remarried and is seeking Christian fellowship or church membership, nothing can be done about the remarriage except to receive that person redemptively. But how do you propose to apply this attitude *before* the fact? Suppose a Christian previously married to another Christian wants your opinion on remarriage? She tells you she was divorced from her Christian husband on grounds other than *porneia* and now has thoughts of remarriage because she finds it difficult to control her sexual feelings. What will you tell her?"

Consider, if you will, Dianne's situation. Only twenty-eight years old, Dianne is a lovely, personable Christian woman.

Her husband had become a Christian a few years before they came in for marriage counseling, and yet he continued to bring serious hangups into his Christian life—a contempt for women and a fear of domination by them. Finally, out of desperation for her physical safety and emotional well-being, Dianne divorced him. Since the divorce, he appears to have made no effort to change.

Right now Dianne doesn't care about male companionship. She confesses that she is "gun-shy." And the men who are interested in her either have hangups or are on the make. They turn her off. "I feel safe right now," she told me, trying to force a smile. "It's easy for me to say that I won't commit the sin of adultery by going to bed with someone or by remarrying. But I know that I'm vulnerable. If 'Mr. Right' should come along, I know that I'll melt."

Dianne is indeed vulnerable. Any man ought to be able to see it. She's not sexually vulnerable—at least not right now. She's vulnerable as a *person*. For years, her husband had verbally and physically beaten her down, taking over the role her father had played when she had lived at home. Though she is personable and attractive, her self-image has been badly damaged. If virtually any man were to come into her life and say, "You're a worthwhile person who deserves more out of life; your needs and interests are as important as mine," she would melt.

A Christian man or woman who separates or divorces is not about to say, "This redemptive attitude is great. I can just jump into another relationship whenever I want and know that I'm forgiven." Dianne's observation on this point was astute. "I can be very pious right now," she said, looking me in the eye, "and say that I think this 'redemptive attitude' is terrible. I could easily say that it encourages people to be indifferent to the sin of adultery. But what happens when I meet a man who makes me feel alive again? How strong will my convictions be then?"

Dianne is doing some realistic thinking. A sincere Christian can never use forgiveness or the security of salvation as a license to sin. He cannot grieve the Holy Spirit, the One who keeps his salvation secure, by saying, "Free from the law / O happy condition / Now I can sin / For there is permission." Explaining this point in Ephesians 4:30, Paul writes, "Do not grieve the Holy Spirit of God, by whom you were sealed for the day of redemption."

For the sake of illustration, let's suppose that even though Dianne is aware of the subtleties of sin and the process whereby people in her position decide to sin, when "Mr. Right" comes along, he tugs at her heart and makes her feel alive. She then falls into deep conflict with her convictions: "God, I don't want to sin by marrying him, but I feel alive when I'm with him." When they're together, they feel fulfilled—even spiritually. They encourage, help, and pray for each other, and consequently the spiritual issues become even more confused. "If marrying him would be such a sin," she asks, "how come I can feel so alive as a person and close to God?"

Although they have been sexually restrained, the pressure grows. Just holding hands and looking deeply into each other's eyes is enough to make their hearts race. They've had enough experience at romance and love-making to know what that look means. Even though a voice inside screams "This can't be," it is happening.

One night in a burst of passion, their convictions are over-ruled. Adultery scores 1, morality scores 0. In agony, they confess their sin to each other and to God. Out of the sincere desire to honor their convictions, they then decide not to see each other for a while.

Their days apart are tedious. They find it tremendously difficult to put each other out of mind and out of heart. No matter how much they pray and read their Bibles, the magnetism is there. Finally one of them breaks the silence—and the other one is glad. "I know we agreed to stay away from each other, but I must talk with you." Perhaps their intentions are sincere, but when they meet, that rush of feelings sweeps over them again. Adultery 2, morality 0.

This hypothetical situation shows how the subtleties of human feelings draw a man and a woman together bit by bit. Their convictions against adultery, once strong, erode under the pressure of the relationship. Only after their moral convictions have been repeatedly and consistently violated comes the decisive question: Which is the greater sin—committing adultery without remarriage, or committing the adulterous act of marriage and seeking forgiveness once and for all?

Pastors and counselors who are faithful to Scripture may reply, "Remain unmarried. If you remarry, you'll commit adultery, because you'll be entering a *state* of adultery that will last as long as you are married." But someone in Dianne's position will protest. "Commit adultery?" she will say. "That's my problem right now. I've committed it ten times, and I'm trying to stop it by remarrying."

We must establish here that remarriage, in such a case, would bring an end to Dianne's and her lover's adultery. John R. Martin quotes some helpful words on this problem from J. C. Wenger:

> The question of whether adultery is a state or an act compares somewhat with the matter of being married to an unbeliever. Surely that is a state, not just an initial situation when the marriage began. And for a Christian to marry an unbeliever is clearly a sin by New Testament standards. Yet we recall at once the New Testament permission, yea even counsel, to continue such unions with non-Christians where the unbeliever is willing. Does this imply the right of divorced people to continue their union even when sinfully contracted in the first place?[11]

In a quotation from Howard H. Charles's paper titled "Some Aspects of the New Testament Teaching on Divorce and Remarriage," Martin reports:

> Is a married couple one of whom has been previously divorced for unscriptural reasons living in a state of adultery? To be sure, they are guilty of adultery. The consummation of the second marriage was an act of adultery against the previous marriage but it was also an act which destroyed the validity of that marriage. Where the sin that destroyed the first marriage in the inauguration of the second union has been adequately dealt with it would appear that the second union could be continued without fresh guilt being incurred daily as these two people live together. It must be admitted that this explanation is not a "thus saith the Lord," and where the Christian conscience can find no rest in this solution the only alternative is to discontinue a relationship which to them is sinful. In any case it may be noted

that the expression "living in adultery," which we sometimes use, is not found in the New Testament. [12]

In Dianne's case, remarriage would become the last adulterous act. *But she must acknowledge it to be an adulterous act.* To put it another way, Jesus knows we do not behave perfectly, in or out of marriage; but He demands that when we do sin, we confess it as sin.

You may ask then, "Suppose I have remarried outside the will of God. Isn't that ground for justifiable guilt?" Indeed it is. But what are you going to do with your guilt? Are you going to keep it inside, allowing it to conflict constantly with your religious convictions? Or are you going to deal with it as you would disobedience to God in other areas of your life? Is your remarriage an unforgivable sin? No, for it falls into the category of every other sin and may therefore be forgiven because of Christ's sacrifice on the cross. Certainly deliberate, premeditated sin has consequences, as the life of King David demonstrates. But there is no justification for carrying a burden of guilt for a sin that you think can't be forgiven.

Of course, you can't undo your sin by going back to your original spouse, because then you would be divorcing and remarrying again. And, what's more, it may well be impossible to go back to the original spouse because he may have remarried too.

If nothing you try seems to relieve you from ongoing conflict with your religious convictions, you might want to examine the possibility that either you are playing a guilt game or someone else is putting unjustified guilt on you. Remarriage outside God's will is a forgivable sin. Consequently, the issue for you is not theological guilt. More likely, it is psychological guilt. Intellectually you may know that you're forgiven, but you may still be unable to feel forgiven.

"Why did Jesus put us in such a difficult position?" you might ask. Remember the context of His statements. He was born into Jewish society at a time when people were inventing every imaginable way to excuse their behavior and call it anything but sin. Knowing their rationalizations, Jesus was saying, "Yes, I am placing a hard burden on you, and not everyone will obey.

But when you disobey, acknowledge that it is a sin." Paralleling this teaching of Christ, 1 John 1:7 tells us that when we sin, we should walk in the light—acknowledge that we have sinned. And when we acknowledge that we have sinned, we hold the Word of God to be true and right.

Today divorced people face the same danger that the Jews faced in Jesus' day. They are in danger of dealing with remarriage that is unbiblical by rationalizing or justifying it. Rather than calling it sin and confessing it before God, they choose to feel guilty because they have disobeyed God's command.

Many divorced persons will object to this point. "You put me in a hard place," they will say. "You are telling me either to do without remarriage—something I find difficult to do—or remarry and commit a sin." In response, I will answer that this is exactly the position that Jesus intends to put you in. He doesn't do it because He is unsympathetic, but because He wishes to raise the institution of marriage to the dignity He intends for it to have. If you must remarry against the Bible's guidelines, walk in the light and acknowledge that your remarriage is a sin. Then confess your sin before God and allow Him to treat it as a forgivable sin. But don't ask Him to lower the biblical standards of marriage because you don't want to call yourself a sinner.

To express this principle another way, "Let God be found true, though every man be found a liar" (Rom. 3:4). The meaning of this quotation in the context of Romans 3 is appropriate here. Our sin doesn't thwart the faithfulness of God and the truth of His Word. Rather, our sin actually enhances them by identifying His Word as something high and holy and by demonstrating His perfection. By reducing the Word of God to an easily reachable standard, the Jews tried to take away the majesty of His Word. Far better for us to acknowledge that God is God, that His Word is holy and demanding, and that we are sinners.

Vocal objections may still persist. "How does this raise the institution of marriage to the dignity it once had?" Very simply. When we are put in the place of either obeying God or of committing sin and having to confess our disobedience, we will usually attempt to obey God. And when we attempt to obey Him in matters of marriage, we will work more seriously at keeping our marriage together. This doesn't mean to imply that people who divorce haven't worked on their marriages. Many have. But even secular studies warn against easy divorce and remarriage on this very ground.[13] They say that if we make divorce and remarriage easy, couples will be less inclined to work on a bad marriage.

Anticipating further arguments, Paul wrote:

> But if through my lie the truth of God abounded to His glory, why am I also still being judged as a sinner? And why not say (as we are slanderously reported and as some affirm that we say), "Let us do evil that good may come"?[14]

To put Paul's statement more plainly, "Why am I judged a sinner if God is glorified through this?"

The answer is eloquently stated in the verses that follow. God is determined to demonstrate to proud men that they are sinners. He desires that "every mouth may be closed, and all the world may become accountable to God."[15] *God does not expect us to be perfect. But He does hold us accountable to Him for what we do.* Once again, the Bible states that He is God and that we are sinners.

The redemptive approach, as we have seen, can be a positive step toward being true both to the Scriptures and to the realities of today's world—both before and after the act of divorce and remarriage. Though the believer may divorce and remarry, he differs from the unbeliever in that he confesses that what he has done is sin. To be sure, both the unbeliever and the believer often have a sense of failure when their marriages don't work. But when the believer confesses that he has sinned, he is also confessing that he has sinned against God's pattern for marriage. Romans 3:7 could be rewritten more positively: "Through my sin, the truth of God has abounded to His glory."

REMARRIAGE AFTER DIVORCE FROM AN UNBELIEVER

In chapter 4, I considered divorce and its relationship to both the believer and the unbeliever. Let's now look at the question of remarriage once a believer has divorced an unbeliever. In 1 Corinthians 7:10-15, Paul considers two circumstances.

The Unbeliever in a Happy Marriage

The first circumstance has to do with the unbeliever who is pleased with the marriage.

> But to the rest I say, not the Lord, that if any brother has a wife who is an unbeliever, and she consents to live with him, let him not send her away. And a woman who has an unbelieving husband, and he consents to live with her, let her not send her husband away. For the unbelieving husband is sanctified through his wife, and the unbelieving wife is sanctified through her believing husband; for otherwise your children are unclean, but now they are holy.[16]

Since the Lord had not given instructions that would apply to marriage between believers and unbelievers, Paul, under the inspiration of the Holy Spirit, laid out the necessary instructions. His language is clear. If the unbeliever is pleased with the marriage, the believer is not to ask for a divorce, so that the unbeliever can be exposed to the gospel.

Even so, I cannot emphasize the principle found in Matthew 7 enough, because many believers are flagrantly violating it. The verse reads, "Do not throw your pearls before swine, lest they trample them under their feet." Dr. Martyn Lloyd-Jones makes it clear that the purpose of this verse is to balance what had been said previously about being careful of condemning others. He writes:

> While our Lord exhorts us not to be hypercritical, He never tells us not to be discriminating. There is an absolute difference between these two things. What we are to avoid is the tendency to be censorious, to condemn people, to set ourselves up as the final judge and to make a pronouncement on persons. But that, of course, is very different from exercising a spirit of discrimination, to which Scripture is ever exhorting us.[17]

The Book of Proverbs likewise warns against forcing our witness or God's wisdom on an unwilling listener. "He who corrects a scoffer gets dishonor for himself, and he who reproves a wicked man gets insults for himself. Do not reprove a scoffer, lest he hate you. Reprove a wise man, and he will love you."[18] Again, "Do not speak in the hearing of a fool, for he will despise the wisdom of your words."[19]

It is also important for us to notice the mention of children in 1 Corinthians 7:14. A wholesome atmosphere where the faith of a believing parent is respected by the unbeliever is indeed spiritually wholesome for the children. In a sense, they are "sanctified"—set apart in a wholesome atmosphere that works for their spiritual good. But it is not spiritually or emotionally wholesome for the child to hear the parent cut down as a believer and as a human being. If the unbeliever is contemptuous of the believer and the gospel, the believer is actually casting his pearls before swine.

One may then ask, "What can the believer do if the unbeliever mistreats him or commits gross misconduct?" The principle found in 1 Corinthians 7:10-11 applies in this case: The believer may leave; but the door to reconciliation should be left open, in case the unbeliever who is really sincere in wanting to make the marriage work returns.

The word *sincere* is very important when the believer is examining the actions of his spouse. It is not enough for an unbeliever to *say* that he wants his marriage to work. What does his *behavior* say? Writing about faith and works, James pointed out that it is not enough for a man to say he has faith (see James 2). His faith must also be proved by works. If he is selfish, self-centered, disinterested in working on the marriage, or keeping another woman on the side, he isn't proving what he says by his behavior.

Numerous times in my marriage counseling, a husband (or wife) has come for counseling with his spouse only to give the appearance of wanting to work on the marriage. As counseling progresses, he will then thwart the process. It's also not unusual for a man or a woman to have a lover on the side and expect the spouse to accept it as one of the conditions of "making the marriage work."

Now, what if the Christian in this case says, "Look, I've divorced this unbeliever, but I can't remain single. I need to remarry." Shall he have to bear the stigma of "adulterer" the rest of his life? It would seem that the redemptive attitude would apply in this case, as it would with the Christian described in 1 Corinthians 7:10-11 who can't remain unmarried. Paul, like Jesus, is calling us to the ideal. But what if we fail to meet that ideal? Is there forgiveness? Certainly!

The Unbeliever Who Wants Out of the Marriage

The second circumstance Paul speaks of is that of the unbeliever who wants to get out of the marriage. He writes, "Yet if the unbelieving one leaves, let him leave; the brother or the sister is not under bondage in such cases, but God has called us to peace."[20]

There is no uniform opinion whether being free from bondage means being free to remarry. A great deal of argument has centered on the word *leaves.* What does it mean—divorce or separation? The Greek word for "leave," *koridzetai,* is the same word used in 1 Corinthians 7:11 to mean divorce, with the condition of remaining unmarried. Otherwise, as I noted in chapter 4, Paul would not have laid out the conditions in which remarriage is wrong. In verses 10-15, Paul uses the word *leave* to mean divorce with or without condition. In verse 15, he speaks of divorce with no condition attached. The clear meaning of verses 10-11 is that the brother or sister *is* under bondage—no remarriage. In verse 15, the brother or sister is *not* under bondage—remarriage is allowed. Indeed, the believer who is free of the marriage but not free to remarry would still be under bondage. What's more, if legitimate divorce does dissolve a marriage, remarriage is not prohibited, as in the case of Matthew 19:9 with the sin of *porneia.*

Paul does not elucidate the circumstances of verse 15. He does not say whether it applies only to a person who becomes a Christian after marriage or to a believer who unwisely marries an unbeliever. Paul's teaching applies to the situation as it stands at the moment of divorce—an unbeliever who wants to divorce the believer. It matters not how the believer came to be married to the unbeliever. If the unbeliever wants a divorce, the believer is free of the marriage and free to remarry.

CHAPTER 12

Remarriage: Some
Practical Considerations

Practically everything that's written on the subject of remarriage advises you not to run out and jump into another relationship right away. Mel Krantzler, for example, considers hasty remarriage a major impediment to personal growth.[1] Most attorneys advise the same: Don't get remarried for at least two years. Even then, it may not be advisable because you or your new interest may not be ready.

I am not suggesting that you become a religious recluse. That extreme is as damaging to personal growth as hasty remarriage. Personal growth requires an ability to achieve intimacy with another person without losing integrity as a human being. I use the word *integrity* in terms of your worth as a person. Most marriages and budding relationships founder at this point. One of two extremes is chosen: either integrity is sacrificed for the relationship, or integrity is so jealously and neurotically guarded that a relationship is impossible.

The one-flesh relationship of marriage does not demand the loss of one's identity as a person. It really means a confident sense of one's identity as a person and the ability to contribute to a relationship as a unique person. The task of achieving

/ 149

genuine intimacy is finding that balance in which you are able to meet your own needs without simultaneously interfering with the needs of the other person. The success with which you can simultaneously meet your needs and help that other person achieve his needs will determine the success of the relationship.

This does not mean that the relationship will always be subservient to individual needs. Indeed, for the relationship to work, there are times when one must adjust the fulfillment of his needs for the other's sake and vice versa. When there is a sense of balance, when each is adjusting to the other, the frustration of individual need and the bad feelings that come out of that kind of relationship are kept to a minimum—except in the case of the opposite extreme.

This opposite extreme is the couple who is so determined to adjust to each other that their relationship becomes bland and unfulfilling to both. Each is so fearful of expressing individual needs for the sake of a harmonious relationship that the relationship gradually dies of boredom.

The challenging, sometimes painful, task you will face following your divorce is the fine art of becoming a live human being with individual tastes, interests, and desires. You must also learn to be such a person in close, warm relationships with others. You will need to be open about your feelings and willing to talk about them with that other significant person. You will also need to listen to what that person has to say about his feelings.

THE PROCESS OF SELF-AWARENESS

Learning to become this kind of balanced person requires self-awareness. Ask yourself these questions: *What kind of a person am I? What kind of a person did I attract in my first marriage? What kind of a person am I likely to attract in a new dating relationship and possible remarriage?* Though you may not even be considering remarriage or have anyone in mind at this point, you might benefit from counseling. An experienced counselor will be able to give you valuable insights into your inner self and help you to direct your growth.

Whether you choose to develop your self-awareness on your own or with the help of others, begin by examining two primary areas: your temperament, and your personality. Temperament is basically your moods and how they are organized. Personality, on the other hand, is how your temperament is integrated into a larger behavioral pattern. Though there is some overlap in an investigation of the two, it helps to separate them for purposes of evaluation.

Take a Look at Your Temperament

Self-awareness requires an awareness of your temperament and its predictable consequences. Temperament, like personality, is not an indelible stamp that can't be changed. As I point out in my book, *You Can Change Your Personality*, we resist changes in our inner self. But these changes can take place. We can modify our inner selves to achieve a more harmonious relationship with others.[2] John Powell writes:

> Sorry, but that is the way I am. . . . I was like this in the beginning, am now, and ever shall be . . . is a handy motto and delusion to have around if you don't want to grow up.[3]

Many counselors use the Taylor-Johnson Temperament Analysis to give guidance in the assessment and change of temperament. The analysis measures nine traits and their opposites, as listed below.

TRAITS	OPPOSITES
Nervous (tense, high-strung, apprehensive)	Composed (calm, relaxed, tranquil)
Depressive (pessimistic, discouraged, dejected)	Light-hearted (happy, cheerful, optimistic)
Active-Social (energetic, enthusiastic, socially involved)	Quiet (socially inactive, lethargic, withdrawn)
Expressive-Responsive (spontaneous, affectionate, demonstrative)	Inhibited (restrained, unresponsive, repressed)
Sympathetic (kind, understanding, compassionate)	Indifferent (unsympathetic, insensitive, unfeeling)
Subjective (emotional, illogical, self-absorbed)	Objective (fair-minded, reasonable, logical)

Dominant (confident, assertive, competitive)	Submissive (passive, compliant, dependent)
Hostile (critical, argumentative, punitive)	Tolerant (accepting, patient, humane)
Self-disciplined (controlled, methodical, persevering	Impulsive (uncontrolled, disorganized, changeable)

The test not only measures the degree of adjustment to each of the above traits, but also reveals particular patterns—combinations of traits. Let's examine four of them.

Anxiety Pattern. The primary indicator is a high score in nervousness, reinforced by high scores in the depressive, subjective, and to some degree hostile traits (though the last trait is not always high). This pattern is often found in people who feel inadequate and dependent and have the accompanying feelings of disapproval, punishment, and loss of love.

Withdrawal Pattern. This pattern reflects a person's tendency toward being quiet, inhibited, submissive, and subjective. Indifference is frequently found in this pattern, since people often withdraw to protect themselves against having their inadequacy exposed.

Hostile-Dominant Pattern. This pattern is particularly alienating. High scores in hostile and dominant traits are reflected in this pattern. People with this pattern are controlling and hostile. High subjectivity adds bias to the pattern.

Emotionally Inhibited Pattern. This pattern is evidenced by unsympathetic and inhibited traits. People who have never developed the social skills of expressing feelings often fall into this pattern because they don't feel comfortable with the expression of emotions.

In my work, I see the above destructive patterns emerge repeatedly in typical relationships. For example, I frequently find the Anxiety Pattern in dependent females who are looking for a strong, caring male. Unfortunately the security that the strong, caring male offers carries a price tag that the female ultimately can't afford. How so? Often the "strong, caring male" turns out to be a tyrant.

This pattern is also seen in a competitive male who is extremely compulsive about his performance. He is difficult to live with because he sees his nervous energy and concern for performance as laudable traits and cannot understand why he alienates people with his behavior.

The Withdrawal Pattern is seen in people who tend to be distrustful of warm relationships with others. Often it is the precipitating cause of divorce and stands in the way of resuming warm relationships with others. A person using this pattern continually puts others on trial and usually offers the excuse, "I'm only protecting myself." In order to control another person, the person using this pattern must withdraw, assume a posture of distrust, and force that other person to prove himself.

Sometimes a relationship is established in which the distrustful person is always pulling proof of trust from the other person. And so the other person is continually trying to prove that he is different from the rest of humanity, that he can be trusted. But this relationship ultimately fails because the other person gets tired of having to prove himself.

The Hostile-Dominant Pattern is most frequently demonstrated in situations where the male keeps the female under control by his demands. You may ask, "Why would anyone want to get into a relationship with such a man in the first place?" Initially this pattern is perceived as strength, something extremely appealing to a dependent female who is willing to pay a price for "security."

The trait is not seen in males alone, however. Socially inept men will often marry women like this who offer the prospect of running social interference for them. This kind of man doesn't like to open his mouth in public or fight with the bill collector. But he knows that he can count on his wife to do it. In the end, he too pays a high price for his security in terms of low self-worth and loss of esteem in her eyes. She controls him, but despises him while she does.

The Emotionally Inhibited Pattern may be found in either sex. In women, it is often accompanied by sexual dysfunction. The husband may complain that his wife can't be warm, caring, or giving. The wife may then defend herself by counterattacking that all he ever wants is sex, which may be true. Insensitivity to a person's emotional inhibition can make things worse.

This pattern in men is often accompanied by excessive objectivity. I call it "the engineering temperament." If a problem develops, he solves it with his slide rule or calculator. He leaves out human feelings entirely and can be contemptuous of them. This kind of male often comes across as the "strong, silent type" and provides an excellent blank slate for a woman to write her fantasies on. She can imagine all kinds of good things going on in his mind that really aren't there, and then she is surprised when she finds out later that all the wonderful attributes she credited him with were just her fantasies.

Do Opposites Attract?

In many ways, opposites do attract each other, both in temperament and personality. There are basic patterns of interpersonal push-pull, that is, patterns in which particular personalities tend to "hook into" each other. A person's vague awareness of what he lacks or wants often prompts him to seek fulfillment in someone of opposite tendencies. A highly subjective and emotional person often seeks the stability of an objective, less emotional person. The objective person, on the other hand, may like the colorfulness of the subjective, emotional person. To use another example, a very rigid and self-disciplined person may admire the freedom expressed in the very impulsive person. The very impulsive person, burdened by his impulsiveness, may admire the discipline of the rigid person. Dominant and submissive people tend to admire each other, as do people who are hostile-dominant/hostile-submissive and affectionate-dominant/affectionate-submissive.

Many other contrasts could be drawn with each trait. Generally, it can be said that when the personality extremes are great, what is first viewed as an asset in the other person later is seen as a liability and may become destructive. One's own traits, once seen as needing tempering, are now exhibited with new vigor.

It's important to see not only what traits you think you have, but also what traits others see in you. You may be surprised to find that others see you very differently from the way you see yourself. Discussion of such differences offers the opportunity for fruitful and meaningful communication. It does not require that the other person's view be "correct." It does require, though, that you be willing to understand how that other person arrived at that conclusion and why.

Do Divorced People Tend to Marry Carbon Copies?

Often, divorced people marry a carbon copy of the person they divorced. But it should be said that the sameness does not always lie in the other person. It may lie in the manner of relating to that person.

Take, for example, the woman who is married to an indifferent, hostile, dominant man who lives as though she were not around. She divorces him and is determined to find a different kind of man the next time. Enter Prince Charming. He is thoughtful and considerate, and above all, he communicates. So she marries him. But *she* is not as communicative as she thinks she is. She does to the second husband what she did to the first one: she refuses to communicate her needs. And even though husband number two is very different from her first husband, he seems insensitive to her needs. Why? Because *she* fails to express them. Here, in this type of situation, self-knowledge is extremely important. One can ask the question, *What part did my temperament play in the demise of my first marriage?*

Sometimes a second marriage is a carbon copy of the first, but the sameness is so subtle that it goes unnoticed. For example, John felt very controlled by his first wife. Tending to be quiet and withdrawn, she tried to control him by cold silence and withdrawal. Unable to stand her coldness, he divorced her. The second time around, he was determined to marry a woman who was more expressive. After marrying such a woman, he suddenly awakened to the fact that once again he had put himself in the hands of a controlling woman. Only this time, she controlled him by angry outbursts and tears.

TAKE A LOOK AT YOUR PERSONALITY

How is your temperament organized into the larger behavioral pattern called "personality"? In *You Can Change Your Personality*, I examine the eight personality types. Each of these types has a balanced or adaptive expression and an unbalanced or maladaptive expression. The first word in the hyphenated combination below is the balanced or adaptive expression; the second is the unbalanced or maladaptive expression.

- The Managerial-Autocratic Personality
- The Competitive-Exploitive Personality
- The Blunt-Aggressive Personality
- The Skeptical-Distrustful Personality
- The Modest–Self-Effacing Personality
- The Docile-Dependent Personality
- The Cooperative-Overconventional Personality
- The Responsible-Hypernormal Personality.[4]

Since I deal in depth with the subjects of personality and personality change in *You Can Change Your Personality*, I will refer you to that book for further reading.

COMMUNICATION

Self-awareness, we have seen, is absolutely necessary if you are to form new, meaningful relationships. This involves awareness of temperament and personality. But how do you communicate effectively this self-awareness and your awareness of the other person, and how do you hook into that other person's personality?

Communication is a risky business. Whenever we reveal who we are, we run the risk of being rejected. John Powell advances this thesis in *Why Am I Afraid to Tell You Who I Am?* "Why am I afraid? If I tell you who I am, and you don't like me, that's all I have." To avoid rejection, many people play the game of finding out who that other person wants them to be and then trying to fill that role.

This game can even corrupt the spiritual dimension of a second marriage. Frequently a Christian woman who has been disappointed with the spirituality of the first husband looks for a spiritual giant in the next husband. Knowing what she's looking for, the man she's interested in plays the part to the hilt—acting like a super churchman and family man. He often raises expectations that he can't fulfill in the long run. The woman then becomes disappointed with him, and he becomes annoyed with her expectations.

Your ability to convey your perspective on life to another person is fundamental to good communication. You must be able to do this without the need to prove the correctness of your perspective or defend it. Furthermore, you must be able to permit the other person's opposing perspective to stand beside your perspective.

The following principles are important in good communication:

Maintain Integrity

Your integrity, and the integrity of the other person, must be maintained. I'm talking about the value both people have as human beings. If, for example, I have worth in my eyes and in those of the other person, I won't need to defend my position once it's expressed. This is not an excuse to avoid considering another position, for I must keep my mind open to change. But I need to know that my point of view will be honored while I go through the ticklish process of comparing it to other points of view.

Honor Another's Point of View

It's important to focus on the point of view expressed, not on the facts. I have an emotional commitment to my point of view, and you have the same commitment to yours. Arguing the "facts" will only harden our positions. I will be much more willing to change my point of view if I feel that you truly understand me than if you try to bludgeon me with the facts.

Likewise, if I'm able to reveal my point of view and give you a window to my soul without fear of attack or ridicule, then I'm more likely to communicate. You don't have to agree with my position. Just let me have it as my own, *until* I'm ready to give it up. You certainly may ask questions about my point of view. But make sure that they are honest questions—questions designed to facilitate understanding and not to embarrass or to show how stupid or inadequate my viewpoint is. Remember, ridicule is subtle. You may be able to make me feel that you think my point of view is ridiculous with just a condescending look.

When we thoroughly understand where we are in our inner worlds, we are in a position to decide whether our differences are so great that we cannot possibly relate to each other or whether we are willing to give ground on a specific point in order to get closer together.

Too often communication is verbal warfare: each person is attempting to bludgeon the other with facts. The bludgeoning is an attempt to make the other person give up his point of view. Such a process makes the negotiation of differences impossible, because emotionally we are unwilling to negotiate (we're being beaten into submission) and we really don't know what to negotiate because we haven't understood each other.

You don't need to agree with another person to make him feel heard or understood. But you must make him feel that he's not going to be rejected by you for advancing his view. This is why I believe that sinners were comfortable in the presence of Jesus, the Son of God.

Beware of Crazymakers

Not everyone who says that he wants to communicate really does. But since communication is essential to the development of relations, we dare not refuse.

One way people avoid communication is by "crazy-making"—the strategy of sabotaging communication. In *Aggression Lab*, Bach and Bernhard define crazymaking as "a subtle yet persistent strategy . . . to upset the composure or psychological equilibrium [having your head together] of another individual or group of individuals."[5] Crazymaking cannot be accomplished by the crazymaker alone, however; he needs a willing victim.

Suppose when you begin talking with someone about a problem, that person blows up or becomes extremely upset. You'll probably avoid the subject next time. If this happens, you've been "had" by the crazymaker known as "short fuse." And if you try to talk to "short fuse" about his short fuse, your attempt will explode in your face too.

I don't mean to imply that people who become upset when you attempt to communicate are deliberately trying to "crazymake." They may feel that their desire to communicate is sincere. But the effect, regardless of the motive, is sabotaged communication.

Several other crazymakers are also common. "Derailing" is used when the crazymaker sees a thought developing that he doesn't want to get into and tries to change the subject or distract his victim with movements or facial expressions. "Overloading," another method, can be done in a number of ways. "Command overloading" demands changes so fast that the victim can't keep up the pace. "Idea overload," which is used by the crazymaker when he's losing ground, introduces more ideas than can be handled. The crazymaker bogs down the communication process and then says that the whole issue is just too complex and beyond solution. "Volume overload" involves using more words than the victim can possibly handle. Verbal people are particularly skilled with this method.

If you can't talk about what's wrong with your communication with someone, look for crazymaking. You or the other person may be doing it and not even be aware of it.

COMMUNICATION CHECK LIST

Both you and the person you are involved with should fill out the following communication check list separately and then compare your responses item by item. You will note that you may choose one of five responses: "yes," "sometimes," "no," or a response between "yes" and "sometimes" and between "sometimes" and "no." The responses in between give you an opportunity to qualify your answer a little more.

When you compare your responses as a couple, remember that you're looking for information on how that other person feels. You are *not* to argue whether or not those feelings are justified.

	Yes	Sometimes	No
I feel free to tell him/her what's on my mind.	—	——	—
I feel I am criticized by him/her for the way I spend my money.	—	——	—

I feel that he/she is saying what he/she really feels.	—	——	—
I find his/her voice or mannerisms irritating.	—	——	—
He/she seems to have certain things he/she doesn't want to talk about.	—	——	—
He/she encourages me.	—	——	—
He/she makes me feel appreciated.	—	——	—
He/she seems afraid to disagree with me.	—	——	—
He/she seems to need to control my relations with other people.	—	——	—
I am afraid to disagree with him/her.	—	——	—
I can't be myself when I am with him/her.	—	——	—
I feel that he/she understands me.	—	——	—
I don't feel free to talk about certain subjects with him/her.	—	——	—
I feel controlled by him/her.	—	——	—
I find it difficult to understand his/her feelings.	—	——	—
He/she usually monopolizes our conversations.	—	——	—
I feel that he/she respects my point of view.	—	——	—
I feel comfortable with his/her views on alcohol.	—	——	—
I feel comfortable with his/her views on smoking.	—	——	—
I feel comfortable with his/her religious views.	—	——	—
I feel comfortable with his/her views on sex.	—	——	—

According to a study reported in *Psychology Today,* the two biggest problems confronting people who are considering remarriage are children and money.[6] These stand in direct contrast with those listed in first marriages. In first marriages, the partners' immaturity, sexual difficulties, and personal lack of marriage readiness are ranked as the biggest problems, while children and money are put at the bottom of the list.

Children

Why are children listed as a problem in remarriage? They are a continuing link to a former spouse. Even though you are divorced, certain expectations are still made with respect to your children. You may feel the squeeze between those expectations and those of your new spouse and even, perhaps, a new set of children. A parent placed in such a situation often feels torn between his responsibilities toward his own children and the stepchildren brought into the marriage. Time and distance often complicate things. It may seem almost impossible to be a parent of two sets of children in two different households. Resentments easily build under the pressure of this frustration.

When you are the parent coming into an established parent-child relationship, you discover that longstanding patterns already exist. Often unspoken expectations are made of you. The children know what your role is supposed to be, but you don't know. Not only must you become aware of what those expectations are, but you must also decide whether or not you want to meet them. It takes a great deal of maturity on the part of the parent you are marrying, as well as the child, to consider how *you* want to play your parent role.

This tension sometimes leads to resentment between the stepparent and stepchild. The stepparent sometimes resents the intrusion of the child into the relationship with the new spouse. The stepchild sometimes feels that the stepparent is an intruder.

Another extreme approach on the part of the stepparent is that of becoming overly anxious about being a good stepparent. Marge, who came for counseling distraught over her failure as a stepmother, is a good example. This was her second marriage, and it included two teen-age stepdaughters. Her first marriage had been childless, and so she looked at the second marriage as an opportunity to fulfill her maternal instincts. She really needed to prove that she could be a good mother.

The stepdaughters, sensing Marge's need to be a good mother, manipulated her mercilessly. They discovered that they could get almost anything they wanted by suggesting that Marge would not be a good mother if she didn't go along with them. Fortunately Marge was bright enough to realize that you can't give teen-age girls whatever they want. But she was caught between this realization and the need to be accepted in the role of mother.

I pointed out to Marge that this kind of manipulation is typical of teen-agers and that she was especially vulnerable as a stepmother. If she wanted to be a good mother, she would not let the girls get away with it. Happily, the girls responded well when Marge resisted their manipulation.

Money

Money is also a big problem. Divorce means a significant cut in your standard of living and resentment toward the former spouse can poison the relationship. When you're hard-pressed financially and your husband has to send a support check to his ex-wife, you may find yourself venting your frustrations on him. Sure, you went into the second marriage knowing about this obligation. But living with it is another thing.

If you're a stepparent supporting a new family, you may find yourself resenting having to support children who are not yours. Sure, you knew that children were part of the package in the remarriage. But it's easy to feel "put upon" when things are rough financially.

Housing

Then there's always the housing problem. No matter which way you go, the arrangement may not be completely satisfactory. If you move into your new spouse's home, you may feel like an intruder. If your new spouse moves into your home, you may feel intruded upon, especially if the new spouse's children do not treat "your property" the way you want it treated. Then again, it may not be financially advisable for you both to sell and buy a third dwelling.

Avoiding Conflict

The above-mentioned *Psychology Today* study reports that the greatest danger among the newly remarried is the tendency to avoid all areas of potential conflict. This, of course, makes communication and problem-solving impossible. Like a dangerous symptom in the body that we try to ignore, those symptoms can be ignored only so long. Relationships and people die when dangerous symptoms are ignored.

Spiritual Compatibility

When a marriage between a believer and an unbeliever ends in divorce, there is a tendency to believe that all the problems in the relationship resulted from spiritual incompatibility. I hear divorced people say, "If only my former husband (or wife) had been a Christian, things would have been different."

This solution is too simplistic. The Bible does make it clear that complete harmony between a believer and an unbeliever is impossible because of their spiritual disparity. But spiritual parity does not guarantee a good marriage. Like everyone else, Christians have hangups that I call "spiritual blind spots." These spots are maladaptive expressions of personality which often go unnoticed. Although people may be made aware of these hangups, they are not always willing to change. In fact, they may even use the Bible to justify their behavior.

The rising incidence of divorce in evangelical circles should be enough to make you beware of the idea that a person makes a good spouse simply because he is a Christian. I see the same self-justification and accusations go on in the dying marriages of Christian couples that I see among couples who make no religious profession.

SUMMARY

The content of this chapter boils down to a few basics. Remarriage is a decision that you must make with a clear conscience before God. Beware of simplistic answers to one of the church's most perplexing problems—divorce and remarriage. God's creation and the rules that govern it are immensely complex, and God hates a lazy mind. Yours, then, is the task of sorting out what we have examined together for yourself—certainly with God's guidance through His church. But the task is yours. It can't be passed off to some authority to tell you what to do. You must do it. And you can't accomplish it by divining the entrails of a goat or randomly flipping open your Bible to a verse of Scripture for guidance. Your mind is a precious gift of God. He expects you to use it. If I have been able to stimulate your mind in regard to divorce and remarriage, then I have accomplished my task.

Notes

Chapter 2

[1]Mel Krantzler, *Creative Divorce* (New York: New American Library, 1975), pp. 30-31.

[2]Ibid., p. 99.

[3]Ibid.

[4]Maxwell Maltz, *Psycho-Cybernetics* (New York: Bantam, 1973), p. ix.

[5]Philippians 4:8-9.

[6]John Claypool, *Tracks of a Fellow Struggler* (Waco, Tex.: Word Books, 1974), p. 101.

[7]Myron Madden, *Raise the Dead!* (Waco, Tex.: Word Books, 1975), p. 101.

[8]David Bogard, *Valleys and Vistas* (Grand Rapids: Baker Book House, 1974), p. 29.

[9]Krantzler, *Creative Divorce*, pp. 47-48.

Chapter 3

[1]Sandra Kalenik and Jay S. Bernstein, *How to Get a Divorce* (Washington, D.C.: Washingtonian Books, 1976).

[2]*Business Week*, 10 February 1975.

[3]Ibid.

[4]Ibid.

[5]Ibid.

[6]Ibid.

[7]Ibid.

[8]Krantzler, *Creative Divorce*, p. 220.

[9]Louise Despert, *Children of Divorce* (New York: Doubleday, n.d.), p. 93.

Chapter 4

[1]*World Almanac* (Washington Star, 1975).

[2]Deuteronomy 24:1-4.

[3]Deuteronomy 22:22.

[4]Alfred Edersheim, *The Life and Times of Jesus the Messiah* (Grand Rapids: Wm. B. Eerdmans, 1950), vol. 2., p. 333.

[5]Matthew 19:8.

[6]*International Standard Bible Encyclopedia*, vol. III (Grand Rapids:

Notes

Wm. B. Eerdmans, 1939), "Marriage," p. 1999.

[7]D. Martyn Lloyd-Jones, *Studies in the Sermon on the Mount*, vol. 1 (Grand Rapids: Wm. B. Eerdmans, 1959), p. 260.

[8]First Corinthians 7:10-11.

[9]F. L. Godet, *Commentary on the First Epistle to the Corinthians* (Grand Rapids: Zondervan, 1971), p. 334.

[10]H. A. W. Meyer, *Critical and Exegetical Handbook, First Corinthians* (Edinburgh: T. and T. Clark, 1877), p. 202.

[11]First Corinthians 7:12-15.

[12]Allen Verhey, "Divorce and the New Testament," in the *Reformed Journal*, May-June 1976, p. 19.

[13]Stanley A. Ellisen, *Divorce and Remarriage in the Church* (Grand Rapids: Zondervan, 1977), p. 17.

[14]Ibid., p. 18.

[15]Ibid., pp. 18-19.

Chapter 5

[1]Despert, *Children of Divorce*, pp. 32-33.

[2]Krantzler, *Creative Divorce*, p. 204.

[3]Ibid., pp. 208-9.

Chapter 6

[1]Everett Shostrom, *Man the Manipulator* (New York: Bantam, 1968).

[2]Despert, *Children of Divorce*, p. 116.

[3]Peter Wyden and Barbara Wyden, *Growing Up Straight* (New York: Stein and Day, 1968), pp. 61-62.

[4]Ibid., pp. 62-63.

[5]Despert, *Children of Divorce*, p. 56.

[6]Ibid.

Chapter 7

[1]Krantzler, *Creative Divorce*, p. 75.

[2]Jay Kuten, *Coming Together–Coming Apart* (New York: Macmillan, 1974), p. 173.

[3]Krantzler, *Creative Divorce*, pp. 38-39.

[4]Bruce Narramore and Bill Counts, *Freedom From Guilt* (Irvine, Calif.: Harvest House, 1974), "Guilt Games," pp. 28-33.

Chapter 8

[1]Suzanne Gordon, "Lonely in America," in *Book Digest* (June 1976, p. 144.)

[2]James C. Coleman, *Abnormal Psychology and Modern Life* (Glenview,

Ill.: Scott, Foresman, 1972), p. 108.

[3]Daniel Sugarman, *The Search for Serenity* (New York: Macmillan, n.d.), p. 82.

[4]Terri Schultz, "Why Two People End Up Lonely, Bitter—Even in a Double Bed," in *New Woman*, April 1977.

[5]Terri Schultz, "Being Alone Without Being Lonely," in *New Dawn*, April 1977.

Chapter 9

[1]George Bach and Yetta Bernhard, *Aggression Lab* (Dubuque, Iowa: Kendall, Hunt Publishing Co., 1971), p. 39.

[2]Walter Trobisch, *Love Yourself: Self Acceptance and Depression* (Downers Grove, Ill.: InterVarsity Press, 1976), p. 24.

[3]Matthew 22:39; Mark 12:31; Luke 10:27; Romans 13:9; Galatians 5:14; James 2:8.

[4]Romans 10:17.

[5]Bach and Bernhard, *Aggression Lab*, p. 41.

Chapter 10

[1]Carol Tarvis, "Men and Women Report Their Views on Masculinity," in *Psychology Today*, January 1977.

[2]B. Lyman Stewart, "Is Impotence Increasing?" in *Medical Aspects of Human Sexuality*, October 1971, p. 41.

[3]Katerina's last speech illustrates the point:

> I am asham'd that women are so simple
> To offer war where they should kneel for peace;
> Or seek for rule, supremacy, and sway,
> When they are bound to serve, love, and obey.
> Why are our bodies soft and weak and smooth,
> Unapt to toil and trouble in the world,
> But that our soft condition and our hearts
> Should well agree with our external parts?
>
> (V, II, 161-68)

[4]See, for example, *The Act of Marriage* by Tim and Beverly LaHaye (Grand Rapids: Zondervan, 1976); *Sexual Happiness in Marriage*, revised edition, by Herbert J. Miles (Grand Rapids: Zondervan, 1977); and *Intended for Pleasure* by Ed Wheat and Gaye Wheat (Old Tappan, N.J.: Fleming H. Revell, 1977).

[5]Marc H. Hollender, "Women Wish to Be Held: Sexual and Nonsexual Aspects," in *Medical Aspects of Human Sexuality*, October 1971, pp. 12, 17.

[6]Ibid., p. 17.

Notes

7Ibid.

8Second Samuel 13:1-9.

9Matthew 5:27-28.

10Published by Educational and Industrial Testing Service, San Diego, California.

11First John 4:19.

12*New Woman*, April 1977, p. 71.

13Ibid.

14*New Dawn*, April 1977, p. 54.

15Genesis 39:7-12.

16Second Timothy 2:22.

17Herbert J. Miles, *Sexual Understanding Before Marriage* (Grand Rapids: Zondervan, 1972), pp. 132-36.

18Charlie Shedd, *The Stork Is Dead* (Waco, Tex.: Word Books, 1968), p. 73.

19Cecil Osborne, *The Art of Learning to Love Yourself* (Grand Rapids: Zondervan, 1976), pp. 29-31.

20Shirley Rice, *Physical Unity in Marriage* (Norfolk, Va.: Norfolk Christian Schools, 1973), pp. 29-30.

21Walter Trobisch and Ingrid Trobisch, *My Beautiful Feeling: Letters to Ilona* (Downers Grove, Ill.: InterVarsity Press, 1976).

22Miles, *Sexual Understanding*, pp. 137-62.

23First Corinthians 8–11; Romans 14–15.

24Trobisch and Trobisch, *My Beautiful Feeling*, p. 85.

Chapter 11

1Ellisen, *Divorce and Remarriage*, p. 37.

2Ibid., p. 69.

3Matthew 19:8.

4George Ensworth, "This Marriage Cannot Be Saved," in *Eternity*, June 1976.

5Ibid., p. 12. See Guy Duty, *Divorce and Remarriage* (Minneapolis: Bethany Fellowship, 1968).

6Ibid., p. 11. See Dwight Small, *The Right to Remarry* (Old Tappan, N.J.: Fleming H. Revell, 1975).

7Ibid.

8Ibid., p. 12.

9Ibid.

10Ibid., p. 15.

11John R. Martin, *Divorce and Remarriage* (Scottdale, Pa.: Herald Press, 1974), p. 22.

12Ibid., pp. 22-23.

13*Business Week*, 10 February 1975.

[14]Romans 3:7-8.
[15]Romans 3:19.
[16]First Corinthians 7:10-14.
[17]Lloyd-Jones, *Sermon on the Mount*, vol. 1, p. 184.
[18]Proverbs 9:7-8.
[19]Proverbs 23:9.
[20]First Corinthians 7:15.

Chapter 12

[1]Krantzler, *Creative Divorce*, p. 116.

[2]Andre Bustanoby, *You Can Change Your Personality* (Grand Rapids: Zondervan, 1976).

[3]John Powell, *Why Am I Afraid to Tell You Who I Am?* (Niles, Ill.: Argus Communications, 1969), p. 167.

[4]Bustanoby, *You Can Change*, chap. 4, "Getting a Handle on Your Personality."

[5]Bach and Bernhard, *Aggression Lab*, p. 207.

[6]Patrice Horn, "Remarriage: Children and Money Are the Big Problems," in *Psychology Today*, November 1976, pp. 26-27.

Subject Index

Scripture Index

Genesis
39:7-12   128

Deuteronomy
22:22   43
24   43
24:1-4   42,134

2 Samuel
13:1-9   119

Psalms
3:1-2   108
3:3-8   108
10:16-18   108

Proverbs   105
9:7-8   145-46
23:9   146

Isaiah
9:6   50

Hosea
2   48
11:8   48

Matthew
5:27-28   121

5:32   43,44,46,134
7:2   50
7:6   145
19:3-12   43,134
19:8   43,134
19:9   134

Mark
10:11-12   43,134

Luke
16:18   43,134

Acts
15:36-41   46

Romans
3:4   143
3:7   144
3:7-8   144
3:19   144
10:17   104
15:7   103

1 Corinthians
6:1-8   29
7:10-11   44,46,146,
    147

7:10-15   135,145,
    147
7:11   147
7:12-15   47
7:14   146
7:15   147
13   125

2 Corinthians
1:3   50

Ephesians
4:26   80

Philippians
4:8-9   23

2 Timothy
2:22   128

James
2   146

1 John   107
1:7   87,143
4:19   124

Revelation
19:11-21   81

Page numbers refer to citation or quotation of Scripture even though the chapter and verse reference may be mentioned only in footnotes.

/ 174